SALVATION THROUGH PATIENCE & PERSEVERANCE

SALAT AL-GHUFAYLAH

SALVATION THROUGH PATIENCE & PERSEVERANCE

SALAT

AL-GHUFAYLAH

Written by Saleem Bhimji

Edited by Arifa Hudda

Foreword by Sayyid Muhammad Rizvi

ISBN: 978-1-927930-40-3

Written by Saleem Bhimji
Edited by Arifa Hudda

Foreword by Sayyid Muhammad Rizvi

Published by Islamic Publishing House
www.iph.ca · iph@iph.ca

Cover Design and Layout by Saleem Bhimji for Islamic Publishing House

Second Edition

Contents

Transliteration Table

The method of transliteration of Islāmic terminology from the Arabic language has been carried out according to the standard transliteration table shown below.

ء	ʾ	ر	r	ف	f
ا	a	ز	z	ق	q
ب	b	س	s	ك	k
ت	t	ش	sh	ل	l
ث	th	ص	ṣ	م	m
ج	j	ض	ḍ	ن	n
ح	ḥ	ط	ṭ	و	w
خ	kh	ظ	ẓ	ه	h
د	d	ع	ʿ	ي	y
ذ	dh	غ	gh		
Long Vowels					
ا	ā	و	ū	ي	ī
Short Vowels					
ـَـ	a	ـُـ	u	ـِـ	i

Terms of Respect

The following ʿArabic phrases have been used throughout this book in their respective places to show the reverence which the noble personalities deserve.

عزّ وجلّ

Used for Allah (God) meaning
Exalted and Sublime (Perfect) is He

صلى الله عليه وآله

Used for Prophet Muḥammad meaning *Blessings of Allah be upon him and his family*

عليه السلام

Used for a man of high status (singular) meaning
Peace be upon him

عليها السلام

Used for woman of a high status (singular) meaning *Peace be upon her*

عليهما السلام

Used for men/women of a high status (dual) meaning *Peace be upon them both*

عليهم السلام

Used for men and/or women of a high status (plural) meaning *Peace be upon them all*

Terms of Respect

The following Arabic phrases have been used throughout this book in their respective places to show the reverence which the noble personalities deserve.

[illegible]

[illegible]

[illegible]

[illegible]

[illegible]

Foreword

By Sayyid Muhammad Rizvi

بِسْمِ ٱللَّهِ ٱلرَّحْمَٰنِ ٱلرَّحِيمِ

In the Name of Allah, the Beneficent, the Merciful
Allahumma ṣalli ʿalā Muḥammad wa Āle Muḥammad

Just doing a good deed by itself does not guarantee its acceptance by Almighty Allah; it is the intention which gives value to a deed:

﴿إِنَّمَا يَتَقَبَّلُ ٱللَّهُ مِنَ ٱلْمُتَّقِينَ ٢٧﴾

> Verily Allah accepts [the honorable deeds] from the righteous people.[1]

In the case of the ritual prayers *(ṣalāt)*, intention as well as concentration is necessary for its acceptance.

Imām Muḥammad al-Bāqir said:

إِنَّ الْعَبْدَ لَيُرْفَعُ لَهُ مِنْ صَلاَتِهِ نِصْفُهَا أَوْ ثُلُثُهَا أَوْ رُبُعُهَا أَوْ خُمُسُهَا فَمَا يُرْفَعُ لَهُ إِلاَّ مَا أَقْبَلَ عَلَيْهِ بِقَلْبِهِ وَ إِنَّمَا أَمَرْنَا بِالنَّافِلَةِ لِيَتِمَّ لَهُمْ بِهَا مَا نَقَصُوا مِنَ الْفَرِيضَةِ

> A person's ritual prayer is indeed raised [to the level of acceptance] - either one-third of it or half of it or a quarter of it or one-fifth of it, because nothing will be raised [to the level of acceptance] except the parts in which one's mind

---

[1] Qurān, Sūrah al-Māʾidah (5), verse 28.

> concentrated. Verily people have been urged to do the supererogatory prayers to compensate for what they have missed [in concentration] from the obligatory prayers.

Abū Ḥamzah al-Thumālī once saw Imām ʿAlī ibn al-Ḥusayn عليه السلام performing the prayers while his outer robe had fallen from his shoulders. The Imām عليه السلام did not pull the robe up until he had finished his prayer and so Abū Ḥamzah asked him why he did not pull the robe up to which the Imām عليه السلام replied: "Woe to you! Do you realize in whose presence I was? The prayer of a person is not accepted [by the Almighty] except the part in which one has full concentration!"

Abū Ḥamzah then remarked that "[If this is the case, then] we are doomed!" The Imām عليه السلام replied: "Verily Allah will compensate the [deficiency in obligatory prayer] by the supererogatory prayers."[2]

In this light, the *nawāfil* prayers become an important way of compensating for the lack of concentration in the obligatory prayers - and *Ṣalāt al-Ghufaylah* is one of the highly recommended *nāfilah* prayers. I commend Shaykh Saleem Bhimji for his endeavour in promoting this *ṣalāt* and educating people about it and pray that may Almighty Allah accept this work.

Sayyid Muhammad Rizvi
September 20, 2016

---

[2] The text of this *ḥadīth* can be found in *Tahdhīb al-Aḥkām*, vol. 2, pg. 342, trad. 1415, and is as follows:

عَنْهُ عَنْ حَمَّادِ بْنِ عِيسىٰ قَالَ: حَدَّثَنِي بَعْضُ أَصْحَابِنَا عَنْ أَبِي حَمْزَةَ الثُّمَالِيِّ قَالَ: رَأَيْتُ عَلِيَّ بْنَ الْحُسَيْنِ عليه السلام يُصَلِّي فَسَقَطَ رِدَاهُ عَنْ مَنْكِبَيْهِ. قَالَ: فَلَمْ يُسَوِّهِ حَتّٰى فَرَغَ مِنْ صَلَاتِهِ. قَالَ: فَسَأَلْتُهُ عَنْ ذٰلِكَ فَقَالَ: وَيْحَكَ أَ تَدْرِي بَيْنَ يَدَيْ مَنْ كُنْتُ؟ إِنَّ الْعَبْدَ لَا تُقْبَلُ مِنْهُ صَلَاةٌ إِلَّا مَا أَقْبَلَ مِنْهَا. فَقُلْتُ: جُعِلْتُ فِدٰاكَ هَلَكْنَا! فَقَالَ: كَلَّا إِنَّ اللّٰهَ تَعَالىٰ يُتَمِّمُ ذٰلِكَ بِالنَّوَافِلِ.

Introduction

By the Author

When we glance through the spiritual regiment of a Muslim, we see that it is composed of various acts of devotion towards Allah ﷻ. Some of these are obligatory and must be performed – such as fasting during the month of Ramaḍān, the 'religious tax' *(khums)* on one's excess net savings, the five daily official prayers *(ṣalāt)* and the major pilgrimage *(ḥajj)* to Mecca. Other acts are highly recommended and have been emphasized by the leaders of the faith - actions such as the minor pilgrimage *('umrāh)*, recommended charity *(ṣadaqah)*, and the optional *(mustaḥabb)* prayers. Ṣalāt al-Ghufaylah is one of these highly recommended and "easy" to perform for those who have earned the Divine providence *(tawfīq)* to implement it into their spiritual program.

This book, *Salvation Through Patience and Perseverance: Ṣalāt al-Ghufaylah,* is our latest endeavour to elucidate upon the jurisprudence of Islām in the realm of the *ṣalāt,* while striving to present such acts of worship in a clear and easy to understand language,[3] and at the same time, expounding on the philosophy, wisdom, and etiquette of these acts of worship which we sometimes perform out of habit or ritual without studying their spiritual aspects.

What follows in this book is the first ever comprehensive analysis in English about one of the most important recommended prayers in Islām - *Ṣalāt al-Ghufaylah* - a joint recommendation

---

[3] Our first project was *Ṣalāt al-Ayāt* - the special prayers performed during natural events such as earthquakes, solar, and lunar eclipses, etc. Published by the Islamic Humanitarian Service (www.al-haqq.com) and co-published by the Islamic Publishing House (www.iph.ca).

from at least two of the Infallibles. The final Messenger, Muḥammad al-Muṣṭafā ﷺ taught us the importance of recommended prayers in general, and specifically the ones between *Maghrib* and *'Ishā'*; and it was the 6th Imām, Jaʿfar ibn Muḥammad al-Ṣādiq ؑ, born on the same day as Prophet Muḥammad ﷺ - the 17th of the month of Rabīʿ al-Awwal - but 72 years later, who taught us one of the specific methods of *Ṣalāt al-Ghufaylah* which not only carries with it a high reward, but also a profound way to change the course of our lives when done with a thorough understanding.

Although the prayer itself is only two *rakʿat* and can be performed in five minutes or less, there is truly an ocean of spiritual benefit and lessons to learn and implement when we take the time to study the contents of what is being recited and the deeper understandings of each word which is uttered. Therefore, one needs to carefully read, study and reflect over the commentary of the verses used in this prayer (as presented in this book and described in various other authoritative works), and also study the life history of one of the Prophets of Allah by the name of Yūnus ؑ (Jonah), if we truly wish to turn our own lives around and turn back to complete servitude of Allah ﷻ - like this great Prophet of Allah ﷻ did.

This book will take the reader through a journey into various areas of Islāmic teachings which may at first seem trivial, however when looked at from a holistic point of view, one will realize that performance of any act of worship in Islām requires the studying and understanding of multiple disciplines, since these acts of worship are not given to us as 'individual' acts of worship - they are multi-dimensional.

It is for this reason that before we even begin to discuss the method of its performance, we need to educate ourselves with the overlying concept of ṣalāt.

From there, the importance of spending time on personal development through acts of worship which are not obligatory upon us, but highly recommended *(mustaḥabb)* - such as the optional prayers.

Once we have understood the importance of going above and beyond what is required from us, we are then able to better appreciate what *Ṣalāt al-Ghufaylah* is, how it was taught to us, how to perform it, and all the periphery discussions in this regard.

Since this prayer is formulated around two main concepts - the forgiveness of Allah ﷻ in our lives, and the All-Encompassing Knowledge of Allah ﷻ - we will also delve into the commentary of the two verses which are recited in this *ṣalāt* because without knowing what Prophet Yūnus عليه السلام went through in his mission and what form his repentance took, it will be difficult for us to appreciate our life challenges and how we can work on altering our conditions.

In addition, we also need to delve into the comprehensive knowledge of Allah ﷻ to better appreciate our role as servants and how vast His forgiveness is.

We then present two other prayers which are highly recommended to be recited between *Ṣalāt al-Maghrib* and *'Ishā'*, and some general jurisprudential issues regarding the recommended prayers.

We conclude by recounting some final points on the life of Prophet Yūnus عليه السلام which give us further inspiration for our own struggles.

From that point, we then present a response regarding an issue which has circulated within some segments of the Muslim community which orators have been inappropriately attributing to the Infallibles عليهم السلام in relation to the spiritual power of *Ṣalāt al-Ghufaylah* and how it relates to the perpetrators of the tragic events of Kerbalā'. This falsified story, as you will read, seeks to exonerate the role of the guilty individuals in the massacre of Imām Ḥusayn ibn 'Alī عليه السلام and his family and friends.

To round up this work, we quote the entire section of the Old Testament of the Bible and the Book of Jonah for readers to be able to compare the Qurānic and Islāmic narrative with what is found in the Bible.

As human beings, we are only here for a limited duration, and we realize that we have very little time at our disposal. If we presume that an average person lives for 70 years in the period of being *bāligh*[4], and if we subtract an average amount of hours spent at work or school, and the amount of time sleeping, eating and all the other vicissitudes of life, then we are left with a little over 23 years of actual "free time" - to engage in recreation, pleasure, entertainment, and of course the specific acts of worship.

Average life span 'post-*bāligh*':	70 years
Total number of "days lived":	25,500 days
Total number of "hours lived":	613,200 hours
Time spent at work/school, eating, sleeping and other daily activities:	409,200 hours
Total amount of hours remaining:	204,000 hours
Total number of days remaining:	8,500 days
Total number of years "free time" (if we live to be that old):	23.29 years

With such a short amount of time available at our disposal to work towards Allah's ﷻ pleasure and the attainment of Paradise, we see that time is truly 'flying by' and 'slipping away' from us. Thus, we need to make the most of the 'spare time' in our lives, rather than drowning ourselves in other activities since before we know it, we will be gone from this world - and forgotten. Thus, we need to

[4] What is termed as *bāligh* or the beginning of maturity - for girls this is the completion of 9 lunar years of age, and for boys approximately 12-15 years of age depending on certain criteria.

ensure that we make the most of the time that we have available to build our next life. Therefore, let us ensure that if we are not able to spend a limited number of years in 'prescribed worship,' then we at least make the most of whatever time we have in our lives before that too withers away - not only quantitatively, but more importantly, qualitatively.

We are humbled for the opportunity to have His Eminence, Sayyid Muhammad Rizvi, write a concise introduction for this book, while maintaining his busy schedule. May Allah ﷻ reward him amply for his services to Islām.

This work was accomplished with the support and encouragement of my wife and editor, Arifa Hudda, for her hard work on this project. Indeed, her rewards are also with Allah ﷻ for her devotion in helping to spread the teachings of Islām, as taught by Prophet Muḥammad ﷺ and his noble family.

The funding for this project was done primarily via our Kickstarter campaign[5] and in an astounding three days, we managed to secure donations from generous contributors around the world to help us publish this book. We are truly humbled to receive such support in such a short period of time.

In addition to all the online donations, many other anonymous individuals approached us personally with their contributions, for which we are eternally grateful.

Finally, we would like to acknowledge the generous and continuous support of:

1. *Academy for Learning Islam* (**www.AcademyofIslam.org**).
2. The Mohsin and Fauzia Jaffer Foundation

[5] https://www.kickstarter.com/projects/1357654719/salvation-through-patience-and-perserverance.

3. *The World Federation of Khoja Shia Ithna-Asheri Muslim Communities* (**www.world-federation.org**) for their contribution towards the printing and distribution of this work within the United Kingdom.

4. *Organization of North American Shia Ithna-Asheri Muslim Communities* - NASIMCO (**www.nasimco.org**) towards bearing the shipping expenditures and assistance of their office staff to ensure that copies of this book were sent to member communities across Canada and the United States of America.[6]

We ask Allah ﷻ to reward all the donors and institutions, and to bless their family and loved ones, and to shower their deceased family and friends with His special mercy.

Keeping the readership of this book in mind, we have done our best to maintain English terminology for the Islāmic terms used but have also used their Arabic equivalent in parentheses to further acquaint the readers with these terms. When it comes to the names of the Prophets and saints, we have maintained their Arabic names and included a glossary at the back of the book providing their Anglicized equivalents.

We ask the readers to overlook any spelling or typographical errors in this book, and to inform us via e-mail if you find any errors so that these may be corrected for an online version or future printings.

Finally, when you - the reader - are given the Divine providence to recite this beautiful *ṣalāt,* we request that you remember everyone who was instrumental in completing this project - namely the author, editor, reviewers, donors and their families, and anyone else. May Allah ﷻ accept all our prayers and grant us that

---

[6] The support of these four organizations was towards the **first** edition of this work. This edition you are reading now is a second edition that is being re-published six years after the initial publication, as we ran out of copies of the first edition.

which we have prayed for others - with no reduction in what anyone is given, for surely with Him are the treasures of the heavens and the earth, and He does not tire in giving to His servants in abundance, nor do His bounties ever decrease by Him bestowing upon His creations.

There is no entity worthy of worship except for You (O Allah!) All glory belongs to You; indeed, I was one of those who was unjust to oneself.

Qurān, Sūrah al-Anbiyā' (21), verse 87

Saleem Bhimji
April 24th, 2022 CE
Ramaḍān 23rd 1443 AH
Laylatul Qadr

Ṣalāt al-Ghufaylah

The Daily Prayers

The most important act of worship and method of connection to Allah ﷻ are the canonical prayers which a Muslim is obligated to perform from the day one becomes of age until one leaves this world - and these are the five daily prayers which must be performed every day in their allotted time span.

In the traditions, Prophet Muḥammad ﷺ has told us that if one's *ṣalāt* is accepted, then all the other acts of worship will also be accepted; however, if one's *ṣalāt* is rejected, then all the other acts of worship will also be rejected. The Prophet has also described the prayers as being the pillar of religion, the means of spiritual ascent *(meʿrāj)* of a believer, and other such beautiful metaphors. Indeed, while in the state of prayer, a believer is in direct communion with one's Lord and it is the time when one is the 'closest' to Allah ﷻ.

The process of gaining spiritual proximity to the Beloved is not only limited to the five daily prayers which are performed at specific times within a 24-hour period; rather, we are told that we can and should speak to Allah ﷻ in this way at any time - not only when we need something, but even to simply thank Him for all of the countless blessings and favours that He has showered upon us, just as the Commander of the Faithful ʿAlī ؑ has beautifully stated:

إِنَّ قَوْمًا عَبَدُوا اللّٰهَ رَغْبَةً فَتِلْكَ عِبَادَةُ التُّجَّارِ، وَإِنَّ قَوْمًا عَبَدُوا اللّٰهَ رَهْبَةً فَتِلْكَ عِبَادَةُ الْعَبِيدِ، وَإِنَّ قَوْمًا عَبَدُوا اللّٰهَ شُكْرًا فَتِلْكَ عِبَادَةُ الأَحْرَارِ

Indeed, some people worship Allah being desirous (Of His reward) - so this is the worship of traders; and some people

> worship Allah fearing (His punishment) - so it is the worship of the slaves, and a group worship Allah in gratitude (to Him) - so this is the worship of the free ones.[7]

Therefore, we have also been encouraged to perform the recommended prayers which have been taught to us by Prophet Muḥammad ﷺ and his noble family, the Ahlul Bayt - not so that we may "buy" our way into Paradise, nor that we ensure our salvation from the Hell-fire; but rather, simply for the fact that Allah ﷻ deserves to be worshipped and cherished for all that He has done, continues to do, and will continue to do for us - in this life and in the next.

Some of these prayers are designated to be performed specifically on a certain day or night within the Islāmic lunar calendar - such as the 1,000 units of *ṣalāt* which are recommended to recite in the blessed month of Ramaḍān;[8] while others take place on special events in specific months, such as on the day of the

---

[7] *Nahj al-Balāgha*, Short Saying 228.

[8] Details can be found in various major books of worship; however, Sayyid Muhammad Rizvi has mentioned the following in this regard:

The special *nawāfil* (recommended or supererogatory prayers) for the month of Ramaḍān are to be recited as follows:

- **1st to 20th:** 20 *rakʿat* (2 *rakʿat* x 10) each night.
- **19th, 21st, & 23rd:** 100 *rakʿat* (2 *rakʿat* x 50) on each of the three eves.
- **21st to 30th:** 30 *rakʿat* (2 *rakʿat* x 15) on each of the ten nights.

The total numbers of the special recommended prayers in the month of Ramaḍān comes to 1,000 *rakʿat*. However, it is important to note that these prayers, from the Shīʿa Islāmic perspective, are forbidden to be said in congregational form *(jamāʿat)* and can only be said individually *(furāda)*.

completion of the fast on the day of *ʿEīd al-Fiṭr,* the completion of the pilgrimage to Mecca on *ʿEīd al-Aḍhā,* or on the birth anniversaries of the fourteen Infallibles. However, if we draw our attention to a tradition from Imām Ḥasan al-ʿAskarī ﷺ and the five signs of a true follower, we see that we have been encouraged to perform a minimum of 51 *rakʿat* within a 24-hour period which is outlined below:

عَلَامَاتُ الْمُؤْمِنِ خَمْسٌ صَلَاةُ الْإِحْدَى وَ الْخَمْسِينَ وَ زِيَارَةُ الْأَرْبَعِينَ وَ التَّخَتُّمُ فِي الْيَمِينِ وَ تَعْفِيرُ الْجَبِينِ وَ الْجَهْرُ بِ بِسْمِ اللهِ الرَّحْمنِ الرَّحِيمِ.

> The signs of a believer are five: praying fifty-one *rakʿat* of *ṣalāt* [per day including mandatory and optional prayers], *Ziyārat al-Arbaʿīn* [of Imam al-Ḥusayn ﷺ], wearing a ring on the right hand, prostration on dirt (*turbah*), and saying the *basmalah*: '*In the Name of Allah, the All-Compassionate, the All-Merciful*' (بِسْمِ اللهِ الرَّحْمٰنِ الرَّحِيمِ) in a raised voice [in the *ṣalāt*]."[9]

[9] *Biḥār al-Anwār*, vol. 72, pg. 75, sect. 24, trad. 7.

The Daily Obligatory and Recommended Prayers	
Prayer	**Number of *Rakʿat***
Pre-Fajr	11 rakʿat – known as Ṣalāt al-Layl
Fajr	2 *rakʿat* before Fajr prayer + 2 *rakʿat* of obligatory Fajr prayer
Dhuhr	8 *rakʿat* before the Dhuhr prayer + 4 *rakʿat* of obligatory Dhuhr prayer
ʿAṣr	8 *rakʿat* before the ʿAṣr prayer + 4 *rakʿat* of obligatory ʿAṣr prayer
Maghrib	3 *rakʿat* of obligatory Maghrib prayer + 4 *rakʿat* after Maghrib prayer (separate from the 2 *rakʿat* of *Ṣalāt al-Ghufaylah*, but it can be combined in the intention according to some of the *Marājiʿ Taqlīd*)
ʿIshā'	4 *rakʿat* of obligatory ʿIshā' prayer + 2 *rakʿat* sitting after ʿIshā' prayer– counted as 1 *rakʿat* standing
Total daily *rakʿat*	Obligatory prayers = 17 *rakʿat* + Recommended prayers = 34 *rakʿat* Total = 51 *rakʿat*

Thus, we see that the recommended prayers are even greater in number - in fact double - than the minimum which Allah ﷻ desires from us, and these are more beloved to Him because their performance shows our devotion and commitment to the faith and its sacred teachings as we are going 'above and beyond' the call of duty to cherish our Creator.

In this regard, there are numerous traditions from Prophet Muḥammad ﷺ and the infallible Imāms ﷺ in which they have accentuated on the significance of engaging in recommended prayers. Below are ten such traditions.

Recommended Prayers in the Aḥādīth

Perfecting the Obligatory Prayers

قَالَ الإِمَامُ الْبَاقِرُ عليه السلام: إِنَّ الْعَبْدَ لَيُرْفَعُ لَهُ مِنْ صَلَاتِهِ نِصْفُهَا أَوْ ثُلُثُهَا أَوْ رُبُعُهَا أَوْ خُمُسُهَا فَمَا يُرْفَعُ لَهُ إِلَّا مَا أَقْبَلَ عَلَيْهِ بِقَلْبِهِ وَ إِنَّمَا أَمَرْنَا بِالنَّافِلَةِ لِيَتِمَّ لَهُمْ بِهَا مَا نَقَصُوا مِنَ الْفَرِيضَةِ.

Imām al-Bāqir ﷺ has said: "Indeed sometimes one-half, one-third, one-quarter or even one-fifth of [the total] of the prayers which a servant performs ascend [into the heavens], because it is only that amount of prayer in which there is focus and presence of heart which will soar, and it is for this reason that the people have been advised to [perform] the recommended prayers so that through this, any deficiencies which exist in their obligatory prayers will be compensated for."[10]

One's Scale of Deeds

قَالَ رَسُولُ اللّٰهِ ﷺ: أَلصَّلَوةُ مِيزَانٌ فَمَنْ أَوْفَى إِسْتَوْفَى

Prophet Muḥammad ﷺ has said: "The prayer *(ṣalāt)* is the scale [which will be used to weigh one's deeds], and therefore a person who performs more *[ṣalāt]*, will benefit more."[11]

---

[10] *Biḥār al-Anwār*, vol. 87, pg. 28.

[11] *Furūʿ al-Kāfī*, vol. 3, pg. 267.

Follow Your Heart

قَالَ الإِمَامُ حَسَنُ الْعَسْكَرِيُ عليه السلام: إِنَّ لِلْقُلُوبِ إِقْبَالًا وَ إِدْبَارًا فَإِذَا أَقْبَلَتْ فَاحْمِلُوهَا عَلىٰ النَّوَافِلِ وَإِذَا أَدْبَرَتْ فَاقْتَصِرُوا بِهَا عَلىٰ الْفَرَائِض

Imām al-Ḥasan al-ʿAskarī has said: "Indeed, the hearts [go into a state] of acceptance and rejection; therefore, when your heart is [in a state of] consenting, then urge it towards the recommended *[ṣalāt]*, and when it is [in a state of] rejection, then suffice it with only the obligatory *[ṣalāt]*."[12]

True Followers (Shīʿā) of Imām ʿAlī

قَالَ الإِمَامُ مُحَمَّدُ الْبَاقِرُ عليه السلام: إِنَّمَا شِيعَةُ عَلِيّ ... كَثِيرَةٌ صَلَاتُهُمْ كَثِيرَةٌ تِلَاوَتُهُمْ لِلْقُرْآنِ...

Imām Muḥammad al-Bāqir has said: "Indeed, the true followers *(shīʿa)* of ʿAlī ... [are known by their] abundance in prayers and their abundance in recitation of the Qurān..."[13]

Keeping Away from Laziness

قَالَ الإِمَامُ جَعْفَرُ الصَّادِقُ عليه السلام: إِيَّاكُمْ وَالْكَسَلَ إِنَّ رَبَّكُمْ رَحِيمٌ يَشْكُرُ الْقَلِيلَ إِنَّ الرَّجُلَ لَيُصَلِّي الرَّكْعَتَيْنِ تَطَوُّعًا يُرِيدُ بِهِمَا وَجْهَ اللهِ فَيُدْخِلُهُ اللهُ بِهِمَا الْجَنَّةَ

Imām Jaʿfar al-Ṣādiq has said: "I advise you to keep away from laziness, as indeed your Lord is the All-Merciful and He accepts the minimal. Indeed, a person may perform a two *rakʿat* prayer solely

---

[12] *Mustadrak al-Wasāʾil*, vol. 1, pg. 177.

[13] *Ṣifāt al-Shīʿa*, pg. 436.

seeking the pleasure of Allah and because of this [short two *rakʿat* prayer], Allah will enter that individual into Paradise."[14]

Spiritually Alive and Dead

قَالَ الإِمَامُ جَعْفَرُ الصَّادِقُ عليه السلام: إِنَّ الْقَلْبَ يَحْيَى وَ يَمُوتُ، فَإِذَا حَيَّ فَأَدِّبْهُ بِالتَّطَوُّعِ، وَ إِذَا مَاتَ فَاقْصُرْهُ عَلَى الْفَرَائِضِ.

Imām Jaʿfar al-Ṣādiq ﷺ has said: "Indeed, the heart [of a person] can be (spiritually) alive and it can also (spiritually) die; so, when it is (spiritually) alive, then coach it with the recommended [prayers]; and when it is (spiritually) dead, then keep it content with only the obligatory [prayers]."[15]

Alleviation of Tribulations

قَالَ الإِمَامُ جَعْفَرُ الصَّادِقُ عليه السلام: مَا يَمْنَعُ أَحَدَكُمْ إِذَا دَخَلَ عَلَيْهِ غَمٌّ مِنْ غُمُومِ الدُّنْيَا أَنْ يَتَوَضَّأَ ثُمَّ يَدْخُلَ الْمَسْجِدَ فَيَرْكَعَ رَكْعَتَيْنِ يَدْعُو اللَّهَ فِيهِمَا أَ مَا سَمِعْتَ اللَّهَ يَقُولُ ﴿وَ اسْتَعِينُوا بِالصَّبْرِ وَ الصَّلاةِ﴾

Imām Jaʿfar al-Ṣādiq ﷺ has said: "What prevents one of you that when a sorrow from the distresses of this transient world visits you - that you perform ablution *(wuḍhū)*, enter the masjid, and perform a two *rakʿat* prayer in which you call upon Allah in these two *[rakʿat]*?! Have you not heard Allah say [in the Qurān[16]]: 'And seek assistance [with Allah] through patience and prayer.'"[17]

---

[14] *Wasāʾil al-Shīʿa*, vol. 3, pg. 30; *Uṣūl al-Kāfī*, vol. 2, pg. 61.

[15] *Mustadrak al-Wasāʾil*, vol. 1, pg. 177.

[16] Qurān, Sūrah al-Baqarah (2), verse 153.

[17] *Wasāʾil al-Shīʿa*, vol. 5, pg. 263.

Total Daily Prayers Should be Fifty-One Rakʿat

قَالَ الإِمَامُ عَلِيٌّ عليه السلام: ...وَكَانَتِ الْأُمَمُ السَّالِفَةُ قَدْ فَرَضْتُ عَلَيْهِمْ خَمْسِينَ صَلَاةً فِي خَمْسِينَ وَقْتًا وَهِيَ مِنَ الْآصَارِ الَّتِي كَانَتْ عَلَيْهِمْ فَرَفَعْتُهَا عَنْ أُمَّتِكَ وَجَعَلْتُهَا خَمْسًا فِي خَمْسَةِ أَوْقَاتٍ وَهِيَ إِحْدَى وَ خَمْسُونَ رَكْعَةً وَجَعَلْتُ لَهُمْ أَجْرَ خَمْسِينَ صَلَاةً...

Imām ʿAlī ﷺ has said: "[Allah, the Most High said to His Prophet ﷺ]: 'I made it an obligation upon the nations which came before (you) that they were to perform fifty prayers during fifty times (of the day), and this was one of the exertions which was placed upon them, however I have lifted this weighty load off from your nation, and I have given them five prayers in five times, and [including the obligatory and the recommended prayers], there are a total of fifty-one *rakʿat*, and I will give them a reward [if they perform these] as if they have performed fifty prayers [as the previous nations had obligatory upon them].'"[18]

Effects of Reciting Abundant Prayers

قَالَ رَسُولُ اللّٰهِ ﷺ: أَكْثَرُكُمْ أَزْوَاجًا فِي الْجَنَّةِ أَكْثَرُكُمْ صَلَاةً فِي الدُّنْيَا

The Messenger of Allāh ﷺ, has said: "Those of you who will have the greatest number of spouses in Paradise are those of you who performed the greatest number of [recommended] prayers while in this world."[19]

---

[18] *Jāmiʿ Aḥādīth al-Shīʿa*, vol. 4, pg. 40.

[19] *Mustadrak al-Wasāʾil*, vol. 1, pg. 175.

For Recommended Prayers to be Accepted

قَالَ الإِمَامُ مُحَمَّدُ الْبَاقِرُ ﷺ: ...وَ إِذَا لَمْ يُؤَدِّ الرَّجُلُ الْفَرِيضَةَ لَمْ تُقْبَلْ مِنْهُ النَّافِلَةُ...

Imām Muḥammad al-Bāqir ﷺ has said: "If a person does not perform the obligatory [prayers], then the recommended [prayers] will not be accepted from him."[20]

Benefits of Stories of the Qurān

When making one's way through the Qurān, the reader is brought face to face with stories of nations and communities that lived thousands of years ago. Some may question the wisdom behind the narration of events which took place so far in the past and which seem to be entirely disconnected from our contemporary lives.

Indeed, there are countless 'stories' mentioned in the Qurān; however, we must appreciate that all of them reflect real-life incidents which have transpired over the course of the history of the world and have affected countless individuals.

Far from being recounted simply as a passing account or narrative, the scholars of the Qurān have gone to great lengths to analyze every story and have enumerated at least fifteen benefits which these 'stories' hold, which are the following:

1. Tranquility in the Heart

﴿وَلَقَدْ كُذِّبَتْ رُسُلٌ مِّن قَبْلِكَ فَصَبَرُوا۟ عَلَىٰ مَا كُذِّبُوا۟ وَأُوذُوا۟ حَتَّىٰٓ أَتَىٰهُمْ نَصْرُنَا ۚ وَلَا مُبَدِّلَ لِكَلِمَٰتِ ٱللَّهِ ۚ وَلَقَدْ جَآءَكَ مِن نَّبَإِى۟ ٱلْمُرْسَلِينَ ﴿٣٤﴾﴾

And certainly, Messengers before you were rejected, but they were patient on being rejected and persecuted until Our help came to

[20] *Wasā'il al-Shī'a*, vol. 3, pg. 20.

them; and there is none to change the words of Allah, and certainly there has come to you some information about the Messengers.[21]

2. Consoling the Soul

﴿فَلَعَلَّكَ بَٰخِعٞ نَّفۡسَكَ عَلَىٰٓ ءَاثَٰرِهِمۡ إِن لَّمۡ يُؤۡمِنُواْ بِهَٰذَا ٱلۡحَدِيثِ أَسَفًا ۝٦﴾

Then maybe you will kill yourself with grief, sorrowing after them, if they do not believe in this announcement.[22]

3. Fulfillment of the Divine Proofs

﴿كَذَّبَتۡ قَبۡلَهُمۡ قَوۡمُ نُوحٖ وَأَصۡحَٰبُ ٱلرَّسِّ وَثَمُودُ ۝١٢ ... وَأَصۡحَٰبُ ٱلۡأَيۡكَةِ وَقَوۡمُ تُبَّعٖۚ كُلّٞ كَذَّبَ ٱلرُّسُلَ فَحَقَّ وَعِيدِ ۝١٤﴾

(Others) before them rejected (the Prophets): the people of Nūḥ and the dwellers of ar-Rass and Thamūd ... And the dwellers of the grove and the people of Tubbaʿ; all rejected the Messengers, so My threat came to pass.[23]

4. Spiritual Fortitude and Determination

﴿ذَٰلِكَ مِنۡ أَنۢبَآءِ ٱلۡقُرَىٰ نَقُصُّهُۥ عَلَيۡكَۖ مِنۡهَا قَآئِمٞ وَحَصِيدٞ ۝١٠٠ ... فَٱسۡتَقِمۡ كَمَآ أُمِرۡتَ وَمَن تَابَ مَعَكَ وَلَا تَطۡغَوۡاْۚ إِنَّهُۥ بِمَا تَعۡمَلُونَ بَصِيرٞ ۝١١٢﴾

This is an account of (the fate of) the towns which We relate to you; among them are some that stand and (others) destroyed ... Continue then in the right way as you are commanded, as also he

---

[21] Qurān, Sūrah al-Anʿām (6), verse 34.

[22] Ibid., Sūrah al-Kahf (18), verse 6.

[23] Ibid., Sūrah Qāf (50), verses 12 and 14.

who has turned (to Allah) with you, and be not inordinate, surely, He sees what you do.[24]

5. A Reminder

﴿وَكُلًّا نَّقُصُّ عَلَيْكَ مِنْ أَنبَآءِ ٱلرُّسُلِ مَا نُثَبِّتُ بِهِۦ فُؤَادَكَ ۚ وَجَآءَكَ فِى هَٰذِهِ ٱلْحَقُّ وَمَوْعِظَةٌ وَذِكْرَىٰ لِلْمُؤْمِنِينَ ﴿١٢٠﴾﴾

And that all we relate to you from the accounts of the Messengers is to strengthen your heart therewith; and in this has come to you the truth and an admonition, and a reminder to the believers.[25]

6. A Means to Reflect and Ponder

﴿وَٱتْلُ عَلَيْهِمْ نَبَأَ ٱلَّذِىٓ ءَاتَيْنَٰهُ ءَايَٰتِنَا فَٱنسَلَخَ مِنْهَا فَأَتْبَعَهُ ٱلشَّيْطَٰنُ فَكَانَ مِنَ ٱلْغَاوِينَ ﴿١٧٥﴾ وَلَوْ شِئْنَا لَرَفَعْنَٰهُ بِهَا وَلَٰكِنَّهُۥٓ أَخْلَدَ إِلَى ٱلْأَرْضِ وَٱتَّبَعَ هَوَىٰهُ ۚ فَمَثَلُهُۥ كَمَثَلِ ٱلْكَلْبِ إِن تَحْمِلْ عَلَيْهِ يَلْهَثْ أَوْ تَتْرُكْهُ يَلْهَث ۚ ذَّٰلِكَ مَثَلُ ٱلْقَوْمِ ٱلَّذِينَ كَذَّبُوا۟ بِـَٔايَٰتِنَا ۚ فَٱقْصُصِ ٱلْقَصَصَ لَعَلَّهُمْ يَتَفَكَّرُونَ ﴿١٧٦﴾﴾

And recite to them the narrative of him to whom We give Our communications, but he withdraws himself from them, so the Satan overtakes him, so he is of those who go astray. And if We had pleased, We would certainly have exalted him thereby; but he clung to the earth and followed his low desire, so his parable is as the parable of a dog; if you attack him he lolls out his tongue; and if you leave him alone he lolls out his tongue; this is the parable of the people who reject Our communications; therefore relate the narrative that they may reflect.[26]

---

[24] Qur'an, Sūrah Hūd (11), verses 100 and 112.

[25] Ibid., verse 120.

[26] Ibid., Sūrah al-Aʿrāf (7) verses 175 - 176.

7. A Greater Wisdom

﴿وَإِنَّكَ لَتُلَقَّى ٱلْقُرْءَانَ مِن لَّدُنْ حَكِيمٍ عَلِيمٍ ٦ إِذْ قَالَ مُوسَىٰ لِأَهْلِهِۦٓ إِنِّىٓ
ءَانَسْتُ نَارًا سَـَٔاتِيكُم مِّنْهَا بِخَبَرٍ أَوْ ءَاتِيكُم بِشِهَابٍ قَبَسٍ لَّعَلَّكُمْ
تَصْطَلُونَ ٧﴾

And most surely you are made to receive the Qurān from the Wise, the Knowing Allah. When Mūsā said to his family: Surely I see fire; I will bring to you from it some news, or I will bring to you from there a burning firebrand so that you may warm yourselves.[27]

8. Truthfulness of Prophet Muḥammad ﷺ

﴿فَلَمَّا فَصَلَ طَالُوتُ بِٱلْجُنُودِ قَالَ إِنَّ ٱللَّهَ مُبْتَلِيكُم بِنَهَرٍ فَمَن شَرِبَ مِنْهُ
فَلَيْسَ مِنِّى وَمَن لَّمْ يَطْعَمْهُ فَإِنَّهُۥ مِنِّىٓ إِلَّا مَنِ ٱغْتَرَفَ غُرْفَةًۢ بِيَدِهِۦ ۚ فَشَرِبُوا۟
مِنْهُ إِلَّا قَلِيلًا مِّنْهُمْ ۚ فَلَمَّا جَاوَزَهُۥ هُوَ وَٱلَّذِينَ ءَامَنُوا۟ مَعَهُۥ قَالُوا۟ لَا طَاقَةَ لَنَا
ٱلْيَوْمَ بِجَالُوتَ وَجُنُودِهِۦ ۚ قَالَ ٱلَّذِينَ يَظُنُّونَ أَنَّهُم مُّلَـٰقُوا۟ ٱللَّهِ كَم مِّن فِئَةٍ
قَلِيلَةٍ غَلَبَتْ فِئَةً كَثِيرَةًۢ بِإِذْنِ ٱللَّهِ ۗ وَٱللَّهُ مَعَ ٱلصَّـٰبِرِينَ ٢٤٩ ... فَهَزَمُوهُم
بِإِذْنِ ٱللَّهِ وَقَتَلَ دَاوُۥدُ جَالُوتَ وَءَاتَىٰهُ ٱللَّهُ ٱلْمُلْكَ وَٱلْحِكْمَةَ وَعَلَّمَهُۥ مِمَّا
يَشَآءُ ۗ وَلَوْلَا دَفْعُ ٱللَّهِ ٱلنَّاسَ بَعْضَهُم بِبَعْضٍ لَّفَسَدَتِ ٱلْأَرْضُ وَلَـٰكِنَّ ٱللَّهَ
ذُو فَضْلٍ عَلَى ٱلْعَـٰلَمِينَ ٢٥١ تِلْكَ ءَايَـٰتُ ٱللَّهِ نَتْلُوهَا عَلَيْكَ بِٱلْحَقِّ ۚ وَإِنَّكَ لَمِنَ
ٱلْمُرْسَلِينَ ٢٥٢﴾

So, when Ṭālūt departed with the forces, he said: 'Surely Allah will try you with a river; whoever then drinks from it, he is not of me, and whoever does not taste of it, he is surely of me, except he who

[27] Qur'an, Sūrah al-Naml (27), verses 6 - 7.

takes with his hand as much of it as fills the hand;' but except for a few of them they drank from it. So, when he had crossed it, he and those who believed with him said: 'We have today no power against Jālūt and his forces.' Those who were sure that they would meet their Lord said: 'How often has a small party vanquished a numerous host by Allah's permission, and Allah is with the patient...' So, they put them to flight by Allah's permission. And Dāwūd slew Jālūt, and Allah gave him the kingdom and wisdom, and taught him of what He pleased. And were it not for Allah's repelling some people with others, the earth would certainly be in a state of disorder; but Allah is Gracious to the creatures. These are the communications of Allah: We recite them to you with truth; and most surely you are (one) of the Messengers.[28]

9. Truthfulness of the Day of Resurrection

﴿وَكَذَٰلِكَ أَعْثَرْنَا عَلَيْهِمْ لِيَعْلَمُوٓاْ أَنَّ وَعْدَ ٱللَّهِ حَقٌّ وَأَنَّ ٱلسَّاعَةَ لَا رَيْبَ فِيهَآ إِذْ يَتَنَٰزَعُونَ بَيْنَهُمْ أَمْرَهُمْ ۖ فَقَالُواْ ٱبْنُواْ عَلَيْهِم بُنْيَٰنًا ۖ رَّبُّهُمْ أَعْلَمُ بِهِمْ ۚ قَالَ ٱلَّذِينَ غَلَبُواْ عَلَىٰٓ أَمْرِهِمْ لَنَتَّخِذَنَّ عَلَيْهِم مَّسْجِدًا ﴿٢١﴾﴾

And thus, did We make them to get knowledge of them that they might know that Allah's promise is true, and that as for the hour there is no doubt about it. When they disputed among themselves about their affair and said: 'Build an edifice over them - their Lord best knows them.' Those who prevailed in their affair said: 'We will certainly raise a masjid over them.'[29]

10. Knowing Allah ﷻ

﴿وَنَبِّئْهُمْ عَن ضَيْفِ إِبْرَٰهِيمَ ﴿٥١﴾﴾

---

[28] Qurān, Sūrah al-Baqarah (2), verses 249, 251 - 252.

[29] Ibid., Sūrah al-Kahf (18), verse 21.

And inform them about the guests of Ibrāhīm...[30]

﴿إِنَّ فِي ذَٰلِكَ لَآيَاتٍ لِّلْمُتَوَسِّمِينَ ﴿٧٥﴾﴾

Surely in this are signs for those who examine...[31]

﴿إِنَّ فِي ذَٰلِكَ لَآيَةً لِّلْمُؤْمِنِينَ ﴿٧٧﴾﴾

Most surely there is a sign in this for the believers.[32]

11. Making Others Understand Realities

﴿فَوَرَبِّ ٱلسَّمَآءِ وَٱلْأَرْضِ إِنَّهُۥ لَحَقٌّ مِّثْلَ مَآ أَنَّكُمْ تَنطِقُونَ ﴿٢٣﴾ هَلْ أَتَىٰكَ حَدِيثُ ضَيْفِ إِبْرَٰهِيمَ ٱلْمُكْرَمِينَ ﴿٢٤﴾﴾

And by the Lord of the heavens and the earth! It is most surely the truth, just as you do speak. Has there come to you information about the honoured guests of Ibrahim?[33]

12. Learning Lessons

﴿وَٱضْرِبْ لَهُم مَّثَلًا أَصْحَٰبَ ٱلْقَرْيَةِ إِذْ جَآءَهَا ٱلْمُرْسَلُونَ ﴿١٣﴾ إِذْ أَرْسَلْنَآ إِلَيْهِمُ ٱثْنَيْنِ فَكَذَّبُوهُمَا فَعَزَّزْنَا بِثَالِثٍ فَقَالُوٓا۟ إِنَّآ إِلَيْكُم مُّرْسَلُونَ ﴿١٤﴾ قَالُوا۟ مَآ أَنتُمْ إِلَّا بَشَرٌ مِّثْلُنَا وَمَآ أَنزَلَ ٱلرَّحْمَٰنُ مِن شَىْءٍ إِنْ أَنتُمْ إِلَّا تَكْذِبُونَ ﴿١٥﴾ قَالُوا۟ رَبُّنَا يَعْلَمُ إِنَّآ إِلَيْكُمْ لَمُرْسَلُونَ ﴿١٦﴾ وَمَا عَلَيْنَآ إِلَّا ٱلْبَلَٰغُ ٱلْمُبِينُ ﴿١٧﴾ قَالُوٓا۟ إِنَّا تَطَيَّرْنَا بِكُمْ ۖ لَئِن لَّمْ تَنتَهُوا۟ لَنَرْجُمَنَّكُمْ وَلَيَمَسَّنَّكُم مِّنَّا عَذَابٌ

[30] Qurān, Sūrah al-Ḥijr (15), verse 51.
[31] Ibid., verse 75.
[32] Ibid., verse 77.
[33] Ibid., Sūrah al-Dhāriyāt (51), verses 23 - 24.

أَلِيمٌ ﴿١٨﴾ قَالُوا۟ طَـٰٓئِرُكُم مَّعَكُمْ ۚ أَئِن ذُكِّرْتُم ۚ بَلْ أَنتُمْ قَوْمٌ مُّسْرِفُونَ ﴿١٩﴾ وَجَآءَ
مِنْ أَقْصَا ٱلْمَدِينَةِ رَجُلٌ يَسْعَىٰ قَالَ يَـٰقَوْمِ ٱتَّبِعُوا۟ ٱلْمُرْسَلِينَ ﴿٢٠﴾

And set out to them an example of the people of the town when the messengers came to it. When We sent to them two, they rejected both, then We strengthened (them) with a third, so they said: 'Surely we are messengers to you.' They said: 'You are naught but mortals like us, nor has the Beneficent Allah revealed anything; you only lie.' They said: 'Our Lord knows that we are most surely messengers to you. And nothing devolves on us but a clear deliverance (of the message).' They said: 'Surely we augur evil from you; if you do not desist, we will certainly stone you, and there shall certainly afflict you a painful chastisement from us.' They said: 'Your evil fortune is with you; what - if you are reminded! Nay, you are an extravagant people.' And from the remote part of the city there came a man running, he said: 'O my people follow the messengers!'[34]

13. Admonition and Exhortation

﴿وَكُلًّا نَّقُصُّ عَلَيْكَ مِنْ أَنۢبَآءِ ٱلرُّسُلِ مَا نُثَبِّتُ بِهِۦ فُؤَادَكَ ۚ وَجَآءَكَ فِى هَـٰذِهِ
ٱلْحَقُّ وَمَوْعِظَةٌ وَذِكْرَىٰ لِلْمُؤْمِنِينَ ﴿١٢٠﴾﴾

And all We relate to you of the accounts of the messengers is to strengthen your heart therewith; and in this has come to you the truth and an admonition, and a reminder for the believers.[35]

---

[34] Qurān, Sūrah Yāsīn (36), verses 13 - 20.

[35] Ibid., Sūrah Hūd (11), verse 120.

14. Servitude to Allah ﷻ

﴿وَلَمَّا جَآءَ عِيسَىٰ بِٱلْبَيِّنَٰتِ قَالَ قَدْ جِئْتُكُم بِٱلْحِكْمَةِ وَلِأُبَيِّنَ لَكُم بَعْضَ ٱلَّذِى تَخْتَلِفُونَ فِيهِ ۖ فَٱتَّقُوا۟ ٱللَّهَ وَأَطِيعُونِ ۝٦٣ إِنَّ ٱللَّهَ هُوَ رَبِّى وَرَبُّكُمْ فَٱعْبُدُوهُ ۚ هَٰذَا صِرَٰطٌ مُّسْتَقِيمٌ ۝٦٤﴾

And when ʿIsā came with clear arguments he said: 'I have come to you indeed with wisdom, and that I may make clear to you part of what you differ in; so be careful of (your duty to) Allah and obey me: Surely Allah is my Lord and your Lord, therefore serve Him; this is the right path.'[36]

15. A Means to Further Knowledge

﴿نَحْنُ نَقُصُّ عَلَيْكَ أَحْسَنَ ٱلْقَصَصِ بِمَآ أَوْحَيْنَآ إِلَيْكَ هَٰذَا ٱلْقُرْءَانَ وَإِن كُنتَ مِن قَبْلِهِۦ لَمِنَ ٱلْغَٰفِلِينَ ۝٣﴾

We narrate to you the best of narratives, by Our revealing to you this Qurān, though before this you were certainly one of those who did not know.[37]

Let us now turn our attention to a specific prayer which is highly encouraged to perform nightly - known as *Ṣalāt al-Ghufaylah.*

Meaning of the term "al-Ghufaylah"

Each prayer in the religion of Islām has its own specific name which is in some way related to that particular prayer.

For example, we refer to the five daily obligatory prayers based on names which denote the time in which they are performed -

---

[36] Qurān, Sūrah al-Zukhruf (43), verses 63 - 64.

[37] Ibid., Sūrah Yūsuf (12), verse 3.

Fajr, *Dhuhr*, *ʿAṣr*, *Maghrib*, and *ʿIshāʾ*, however above and beyond that, each ʿArabic word for these five times also has other unique meanings - such as *Fajr* which literally means 'the starting point,' and also means 'an explosion.' The same holds true for the remainder of the daily prayers, and the meaning of their names.

The prayers on the first of Shawwāl are known as *Ṣalāt al-ʿEid* - the meaning of *ʿeid* is 'to return back;' and the prayer during an earthquake or other natural occurrence is called *Ṣalāt al-Āyāt* - the meaning of *āyāt* being 'the signs [of Allah].'

Lexically, the word *ghufaylah* comes from the Arabic root word *gha-fa-la* which means 'to fall into complete and total heedlessness or negligence;' however in its current structure, it is the diminutive[38] form of the word *ghaflah* - which means 'negligence or neglect.'

Thus, the word *ghufaylah*[39] means 'one who has fallen into a

---

[38] In language structure, a diminutive or diminutive form is a formation of a word used to convey a slighter degree of the root meaning, smallness of the object or quality named, encapsulation, intimacy, or endearment. It is the opposite of an augmentative. Diminutives are often used for the purpose of expressing affection. In many languages, the meaning of diminution can be translated as "tiny" or "wee;" and diminutives are used frequently when speaking to small children; adults sometimes use diminutives when they express extreme tenderness and intimacy by behaving and talking like children. In English, the alteration of meaning is often conveyed through clipping, either alone or combined with an affix, and English diminutives tend to be shorter and more colloquial than the basic form of the word. (Wikipedia - with modifications)

[39] In his book, *Al-Mūjiz fī al-Taṣrīf*, vol. 2, pg. 397, Ali Abdur-Rasheed writes that in Arabic, the diminutive noun signifies smallness or a reduction in size, body, or mass - such as *rajulu* or man, and *rujaylu* or small man. He also mentions that at times, it

complete and utter state of heedlessness;' the *taa* at the end on the word *al-ghufaylah* does not denote that this word is of the feminine tense, rather it denotes an emphasis on this trait being present in a person.

As we will see later on in this discussion, Prophet Muḥammad ﷺ and his successors ﷺ have - for reasons known to them alone - referred to the time frame between *Maghrib* and *ʿIshā'* as the period of 'negligence,' so in order for us to take ourselves out of that phase and to ensure that we do not fall into such a state of neglect of ourselves, this prayer has been strongly advised to perform. Certain key verses, and an important historical figure, Prophet Yūnus ﷺ, and his trials and tribulations and his response to them are remembered at this specific time of the night in this special prayer, as well as the All-Comprehensive Knowledge of Allah ﷻ.

The "Time of Negligence"

It has been narrated from Imām Jaʿfar al-Ṣādiq ﷺ going back to his forefathers who narrate from the noble Prophet Muḥammad ﷺ regarding this recommended prayer that:

صَلُّوا فِي سَاعَةِ الْغَفْلَةِ وَلَوْ رَكْعَتَيْنِ فَإِنَّهُمَا تُورِدَانِ دَارَ الْكَرَامَةِ

> Recite a *ṣalāt* in the 'time of negligence' even if it be a two-unit prayer, and this will permit you to enter the Abode of Munificence (Paradise).[40]

---

can signify insignificance - for example *ʿabd* or servant, and *ʿubayd* or humble servant. It can also signify something which is few, such as *dirham* or coin, and *durayhimāt* or a few coins. Also, the diminutive can signify shortness of time and nearness of a place. Yet another usage is to denote compassion and sympathy and lastly, he writes that there are rare examples where it is used to demonstrate greatness.

[40] *Falāḥ al-Sā'il*, Sayyid ibn Ṭāwūs, pg. 244.

In another tradition from Prophet Muḥammad ﷺ, we read the following:

تَنْفِلوُا فِي سَاعَةِ الْغَفْلَةِ وَلَوْ رَكْعَتَيْنِ خَفِيفَتَيْنِ فَإِنَّهُمَا تُورِدَانِ دَارَ الْكَرَامَةِ. قِيلَ يَا رَسُولَ اللّٰهِ وَمَا سَاعَةُ الْغَفْلَةِ؟ قَالَ ﷺ: بَيْنَ الْمَغْرِبِ وَالْعِشَاءِ

> Perform a voluntary prayer during the 'time of negligence' even if it is a small two *rakʿat* prayer because these two *[rakʿat]* will permit you to enter the Abode of Munificence (Paradise). It was said: 'O Messenger of Allah, what is the time of negligence?' The Prophet, prayers of Allah be upon him and his family replied: '[The time] between *maghrib* and *ʿishāʾ*.'[41]

In a final tradition, Imām Jaʿfar al-Ṣādiq ﵇, quoting his forefathers, quotes the Messenger of Allah ﷺ as saying:

لاَ تَتْرُكُوا رَكْعَتَي الْغُفَيْلَةِ وَ هُمَا بَيْنَ الْعِشَائَيْنِ

> Do not abandon the two *rakʿat* of *[Ṣalāt] al-Ghufaylah* - and this is (the prayer) performed between the two *ʿishāʾ (maghrib and ʿishāʾ)*.[42]

It should be noted that the time between the start of *Fajr* (what is referred to as *fajr al-ṣādiq*) and the actual rising of the sun is also a time of heedlessness - *ghaflah*, however the traditions have not referred to the early morning period with this name, nor have we been instructed to perform any specific recommended prayers at that time of the day. Therefore, whenever we read the term *ghufaylah*, it refers specifically to ANY recommended prayer

---

[41] *Falāḥ al-Sāʾil*, pg. 245.

[42] Ibid., pg. 246.

which is performed between the time of *Maghrib* and *'Ishā'*. However, to truly benefit from this special period of the night and to gain the maximum reward and spiritual ascent which has been spoken about in the traditions, a believer should perform the specific prayer taught by Imām Ja'far al-Ṣādiq ﷺ which we will explain shortly.

In addition, it is clear from the traditions that Prophet Muḥammad ﷺ used to perform *Maghrib* and *'Ishā'* prayers right when the prime time set in; and since in his region the time difference between these two prayers was roughly one hour, we are told that this is a time in which Satan and his legion of followers spread themselves upon the Earth, and try to make the believers fall into heedlessness in regards to Allah ﷻ. Thus, during this period of negligence of Allah ﷻ, it is the best time for a believer to perform this prayer to keep alive His remembrance when others may be falling into the pit of heedlessness of their Creator.

There are some other names which have been used for this period and the recommended prayers to be performed, and these include:

1. The two rak'at of al-ghufaylah.
2. The two rak'at of al-ghaflah.
3. The two *rak'at* at the time of negligence.
4. *Nāshiat al-Layl* which is a specific *ṣalāt* performed in this time frame.
5. *Nāfilah al-Maghrib* – which is a total of four *rak'at* of which the two *rak'at* which are discussed in this book have been highly emphasized to be performed, and 'combined' with the intention of the optional prayers of *Maghrib.*

As we can see, we have been encouraged to perform at least two *rak'at* of *ṣalāt* between the *Maghrib* and *'Ishā'* prayers, but there are multiple recommended prayers which can be performed at that time of the evening. However, there is one specific two *rak‘at* prayer which we have been highly encouraged to perform which has been advised by the sixth Imām and successor of Prophet Muḥammad ﷺ, namely Imām Ja‘far ibn Muḥammad al-Ṣādiq ؑ.

A Form of Ṣalāt al-Ghufaylah[43]

Regarding the method of performing this prayer, we relate the following tradition:

عَنْ عَلِيّ بْنِ مُحَمَّدِ بْنِ يُوسُفَ عَنْ أَحْمَدَ بْنِ مُحَمَّدِ بْنِ مُحَمَّدِ بْنِ سُلَيْمَانَ الزُّرَارِيّ عَنْ أَبِي جَعْفَرٍ الْحُسَيْنِيِّ مُحَمَّدِ بْنِ الْحُسَيْنِ الْأَشْتَرِ عَنْ عَبَّادِ بْنِ يَعْقُوبَ عَنْ عَلِيّ بْنِ الْحَكَمِ عَنْ هِشَامٍ بْنِ سَالِمٍ عَنْ أَبِي عَبْدِ اللَّهِ الصَّادِقِ ؑ: قَالَ مَنْ صَلَّى بَيْنَ الْعِشَاءَيْنِ رَكْعَتَيْنِ قَرَأَ فِي الْأُولَى الْحَمْدَ وَ قَوْلَهُ تَعَالَى: وَذَا النُّونِ إِذْ ذَهَبَ مُغَاضِبًا فَظَنَّ أَنْ لَنْ نَقْدِرَ عَلَيْهِ فَنَادَى فِي الظُّلُمَاتِ أَنْ لاَ إِلٰهَ إِلَّا أَنْتَ سُبْحَانَكَ إِنِّي كُنْتُ مِنَ الظَّالِمِينَ فَاسْتَجَبْنَا لَهُ وَ نَجَّيْنَاهُ مِنَ الْغَمِّ وَكَذٰلِكَ نُنْجِي الْمُؤْمِنِينَ - وَفِي الثَّانِيَةِ الْحَمْدَ وَ قَوْلَهُ تَعَالَى: وَعِنْدَهُ مَفَاتِحُ الْغَيْبِ لَا يَعْلَمُهَا إِلَّا هُوَ وَيَعْلَمُ مَا فِي الْبَرِّ وَالْبَحْرِ وَمَا تَسْقُطُ مِنْ وَرَقَةٍ إِلَّا يَعْلَمُهَا وَلَا حَبَّةٍ فِي ظُلُمَاتِ الْأَرْضِ وَلَا رَطْبٍ وَلَا يَابِسٍ إِلَّا فِي كِتَابٍ مُبِينٍ - فَإِذَا فَرَغَ مِنَ الْقِرَاءَةِ رَفَعَ يَدَيْهِ وَقَالَ: أَللّٰهُمَّ إِنِّي أَسْأَلُكَ بِمَفَاتِحِ الْغَيْبِ الَّتِي لَا

---

[43] A video produced by the *Islamic Publishing House* in English on how to perform this prayer can be found at: **youtube.com/watch?v=TkZOaeznNsg** or by simply typing in the word ‘*ghufaylah*’ in the YouTube search box.

يَعْلَمُهَا إِلَّا أَنْتَ أَنْ تُصَلِّيَ عَلَى مُحَمَّدٍ وَآلِ مُحَمَّدٍ وَأَنْ تَفْعَلَ بِي كَذَا وَ كَذَا - ثُمَّ تَقُولُ: أَللّٰهُمَّ أَنْتَ وَلِيُّ نِعْمَتِي وَالْقَادِرُ عَلَى طَلِبَتِي تَعْلَمُ حَاجَتِي فَأَسْأَلُكَ بِحَقِّ مُحَمَّدٍ وَآلِ مُحَمَّدٍ لَمَّا قَضَيْتَهَا لِي - وَيَسْأَلُ اللّٰهَ جَلَّ جَلَالُهُ حَاجَتَهُ أَعْطَاهُ اللّٰهُ مَا سَأَلَ فَإِنَّ النَّبِيَّ ﷺ قَالَ: لَا تَتْرُكُوا رَكْعَتَيِ الْغَفْلَةِ وَهُمَا بَيْنَ الْعِشَاءَيْنِ.

It has been narrated from ʿAlī ibn Muḥammad ibn Yūsuf from Aḥmad ibn Muḥammad ibn Muḥammad ibn Sulaymān al-Zurārī from Abī Jaʿfar al-Ḥusaynī Muḥammad ibn al-Ḥusayn al-Ashtar from ʿAbbād ibn Yaʿqūb from ʿAlī ibn al-Ḥakam from Hishām ibn Sālim from Abī ʿAbdillah al-Ṣādiq, peace be upon him, that he said: "A person who recites a two *rakʿat* prayer between the two *ʿishāʾ (maghrib and ʿishāʾ)*, and in the first (*rakʿat*) he recites [Sūrah] al-Ḥamd, and then His [Allah's] words [from the Qurān], the Most High: 'And the Man of the Fish (Prophet Yūnus), when he left in a rage, thinking that We would not put him to hardship. Then he cried out in the darkness, 'There is no god except You! You are immaculate! I have indeed been among the wrongdoers!' So, We answered his prayer and delivered him from the agony; and thus, do We deliver the faithful.' Then in the second *[rakʿat]*, one recites [Sūrah] al-Ḥamd followed by His words, the Highest: 'With Him are the treasures of the Unseen; no one knows them except Him. He knows whatever there is in the land and the sea. No leaf falls without Him knowing it, nor is there a grain in the darkness of the earth, nor anything fresh or withered but it is in a manifest Book.' After finishing this recitation, one should lift the hands [in the position of *qunūt*] and say: 'O Allah, I beseech You in the name of the Keys of the Invisible (world) that no one knows except for You; send blessings upon Muḥammad and his Household,' **then mention one's needs,** then one should conclude by saying: 'O Allah, You are the source of the graces that I have, You have the power to respond to my request, and You know my needs; I therefore beseech You in the name of Muḥammad and his Household, peace be upon him and them, to grant me my needs. If a person [sincerely] asks Allah, Grandeur and Greatness be to Him, for one's requests, then Allah will grant that person whatever one asks for as indeed the Prophet, prayers of Allah be upon him and his family, has said: 'Do not refrain from [performing] the two *rak'at* of *al-ghaflah*, and this is between the two *'Ishā' [Maghrib and 'Ishā']*.'"[44]

Thus, the methods and the importance of this specific prayer which the believers are highly encouraged to perform every evening come directly to us from the seat of the Divine mission; the ones to whom the Angels turn to; the destination of the Divine revelation; the originating source of mercy; the treasures of knowledge (of the Prophet); the ultimate in forbearance; the foundation of generosity and the leaders of the entire world - namely the Ahlul Bayt 🕮.

Ṣalāt al-Ghufaylah - Step by Step

The method for performing *Ṣalāt al-Ghufaylah* is identical according to the rulings of all the senior scholars of Islām *(marāji' taqlīd)* and what we present here are the step-by-step details on how to perform this prayer.

After completing the *Maghrib* prayers (ideally right when the time for it sets in) and its *ta'qibāt*, one should stand up, make an

---

[44] *Mustadrak al-Wasā'il al-Shī'a*, vol. 6, pg. 304, tradition 6875.

intention for performing the *nāfilah* of *Maghrib*, and within that, *Ṣalāt al-Ghufaylah*, and perform the following steps:

Takbīratul Iḥrām to start the ṣalāt	
	ٱللَّهُ أَكۡبَرُ

↓

First *Rakʿat* - Sūrah al-Fātiḥa	
	﴿بِسۡمِ ٱللَّهِ ٱلرَّحۡمَٰنِ ٱلرَّحِيمِ ١ ٱلۡحَمۡدُ لِلَّهِ رَبِّ ٱلۡعَٰلَمِينَ ٢ ٱلرَّحۡمَٰنِ ٱلرَّحِيمِ ٣ مَٰلِكِ يَوۡمِ ٱلدِّينِ ٤ إِيَّاكَ نَعۡبُدُ وَإِيَّاكَ نَسۡتَعِينُ ٥ ٱهۡدِنَا ٱلصِّرَٰطَ ٱلۡمُسۡتَقِيمَ ٦ صِرَٰطَ ٱلَّذِينَ أَنۡعَمۡتَ عَلَيۡهِمۡ غَيۡرِ ٱلۡمَغۡضُوبِ عَلَيۡهِمۡ وَلَا ٱلضَّآلِّينَ ٧﴾

↓

First *Rakʿat* - Sūrah al-Anbiyāʾ (21), Verses 87 and 88[45]

---

[45] The tradition does not mention that we need to start the recitation of this verse, and the verse in the second *rakʿat* with the *basmalah* (بِسْمِ اللَّهِ الرَّحْمَنِ الرَّحِيمِ). In addition, there is no recommendation of starting such recitations of individual verses with the *basmalah*, and as such although it is permissible to be done, if one does so with the intention of it beginning the recitation of the Qurān and for earning His pleasure, then one should not do so with an intention of it being a part of the religious teachings of Islam.

﴿وَذَا ٱلنُّونِ إِذ ذَّهَبَ مُغَٰضِبٗا فَظَنَّ أَن لَّن نَّقۡدِرَ عَلَيۡهِ
فَنَادَىٰ فِي ٱلظُّلُمَٰتِ أَن لَّآ إِلَٰهَ إِلَّآ أَنتَ سُبۡحَٰنَكَ إِنِّي
كُنتُ مِنَ ٱلظَّٰلِمِينَ ٨٧ فَٱسۡتَجَبۡنَا لَهُۥ وَنَجَّيۡنَٰهُ مِنَ
ٱلۡغَمِّۚ وَكَذَٰلِكَ نُـۨجِي ٱلۡمُؤۡمِنِينَ ٨٨﴾

First *Rakʿat* - *Takbīr* before *Rukūʿ*

أَللّٰهُ أَكْبَرُ

First Rakʿat - Rukūʿ

سُبْحَانَ اللهِ سُبْحَانَ اللهِ سُبْحَانَ اللهِ

Or one may say:

سُبْحَانَ رَبِّيَ الْعَظِيمِ وَبِحَمْدِهِ

First *Rakʿat* - Standing Before *Sajdah*

سَمِعَ اللهُ لِـمَنْ حَمِدَهُ

First Rakʿat - Takbīr Before Sajdah	
	أَللّٰهُ أَكْبَرُ

↓

First *Rakʿat* - First *Sajdah*	
	سُبْحَانَ اللّٰهِ سُبْحَانَ اللّٰهِ سُبْحَانَ اللّٰهِ Or one may say: سُبْحَانَ رَبِّيَ الأَعْلَى وَبِحَمْدِهِ

↓

First Rakʿat - Jalsa	
	أَللّٰهُ أَكْبَرُ. أَسْتَغْفِرُ اللّٰهِ رَبِي وَ أَتُوبُ إِلَيْهِ. أَللّٰهُ أَكْبَرُ

↓

First *Rakʿat* - Second *Sajdah*	
	سُبْحَانَ اللّٰهِ سُبْحَانَ اللّٰهِ سُبْحَانَ اللّٰهِ Or one may say: سُبْحَانَ رَبِّيَ الأَعْلَى وَبِحَمْدِهِ

↓

Completion of First *Rakʿat*

أَللهُ أَكْبَرُ

Standing up to start the Second *Rakʿat*

Recite as you stand up:

بِحَوْلِ اللهِ وَ قُوَّتِهِ أَقُومُ وَ أَقْعُدُ

Second *Rakʿat* - Sūrah al-Fātiḥa

﴿بِسۡمِ ٱللَّهِ ٱلرَّحۡمَٰنِ ٱلرَّحِيمِ ١ ٱلۡحَمۡدُ لِلَّهِ رَبِّ
ٱلۡعَٰلَمِينَ ٢ ٱلرَّحۡمَٰنِ ٱلرَّحِيمِ ٣ مَٰلِكِ يَوۡمِ
ٱلدِّينِ ٤ إِيَّاكَ نَعۡبُدُ وَإِيَّاكَ نَسۡتَعِينُ ٥ ٱهۡدِنَا
ٱلصِّرَٰطَ ٱلۡمُسۡتَقِيمَ ٦ صِرَٰطَ ٱلَّذِينَ أَنۡعَمۡتَ
عَلَيۡهِمۡ غَيۡرِ ٱلۡمَغۡضُوبِ عَلَيۡهِمۡ وَلَا ٱلضَّآلِّينَ
٧﴾

Second *Rakʿat* - Sūrah al-Anʿām (6), Verse 59

﴿وَعِندَهُۥ مَفَاتِحُ ٱلۡغَيۡبِ لَا يَعۡلَمُهَآ إِلَّا هُوَۚ وَيَعۡلَمُ
مَا فِي ٱلۡبَرِّ وَٱلۡبَحۡرِۚ وَمَا تَسۡقُطُ مِن وَرَقَةٍ إِلَّا

	يَعْلَمُهَا وَلَا حَبَّةٍ فِي ظُلُمَٰتِ ٱلْأَرْضِ وَلَا رَطْبٍ وَلَا يَابِسٍ إِلَّا فِي كِتَٰبٍ مُّبِينٍ ﴿٥٩﴾

↓

Second *Rakʿat* - *Takbīr* before going into *Qunūt*	
	اَللّٰهُ أَكْبَرُ

↓

Second *Rakʿat* - *Qunūt* - Part One	
	أَللّٰهُمَّ إِنِّي أَسْئَلُكَ بِمَفَاتِحِ الْغَيْبِ الَّتِى لاَ يَعْلَمُهَا إِلاَّ أَنْتَ أَنْ تُصَلِّيَ عَلٰى مُحَمَّدٍ وَ آلِ مُحَمَّدٍ وَ أَنْ تَفْعَلَ بِي...

↓

Second *Rakʿat* - *Qunūt* - Part Two	
	At this stage, ask your legitimate wishes and desires from Allah in ANY language you wish.

↓

Second *Rakʿat* - *Qunūt* - Part Three	
	أَللّٰهُمَّ أَنْتَ وَلِيُّ نِعْمَتِى وَالْقَادِرُ عَلٰى طَلِبَتِى تَعْلَمُ حَاجَتِى فَأَسْئَلُكَ بِحَقِّ مُحَمَّدٍ وَ آلِ مُحَمَّدٍ عَلَيْهِ وَ عَلَيْهِمُ السَّلاَمُ لَمَّا قَضَيْتَهَا لِي

↓

Second *Rakʿat* - *Takbīr* before going into *Rukūʿ*

أَللهُ أَكْبَرُ

Second Rakʿat - Rukūʿ

سُبْحَانَ اللهِ سُبْحَانَ اللهِ سُبْحَانَ اللهِ

Or one may say:

سُبْحَانَ رَبِّيَ الْعَظِيمِ وَبِحَمْدِهِ

Second *Rakʿat* - Standing before going into *Sajdah*

سَمِعَ اللهُ لِمَنْ حَمِدَهُ

Second *Rakʿat* - *Takbīr* before going into *Sajdah*

أَللهُ أَكْبَرُ

Second *Rakʿat* - First *Sajdah*	
	سُبْحَانَ اللهِ سُبْحَانَ اللهِ سُبْحَانَ اللهِ Or one may say: سُبْحَانَ رَبِّيَ الأَعْلَى وَبِحَمْدِهِ

↓

Second Rakʿat - Jalsa	
	أَللهُ أَكْبَرُ. أَسْتَغْفِرُ اللهِ رَبِي وَ أَتُوبُ إِلَيْهِ. أَللهُ أَكْبَرُ

↓

Second *Rakʿat* - Second *Sajdah*	
	سُبْحَانَ اللهِ سُبْحَانَ اللهِ سُبْحَانَ اللهِ Or one may say: سُبْحَانَ رَبِّيَ الأَعْلَى وَبِحَمْدِهِ

↓

Second Rakʿat - Takbīr before Tashahhud and Salām	
	أَللهُ أَكْبَرُ

↓

Second Rak'at - Tashahhud	
	أَشْهَدُ أَنْ لاَ إِلَهَ اِلاَّ اللهُ وَحْدَهُ لاَ شَرِيكَ لَهُ وَأَشْهَدُ أَنَّ مُحَمَّداً عَبْدُهُ وَرَسُولُهُ. أَللَّهُمَّ صَلِّ عَلَى مُحَمَّدٍ وَّآلِ مُحَمَّدٍ.

↓

Second Rak'at - Salām	
	أَلسَّلاَمُ عَلَيْكَ أَيُّهَا النَّبِيُّ وَرَحْمَةُ اللهِ وَبَرَكَاتُهُ. أَلسَّلاَمُ عَلَيْنَا وَعَلَى عِبَادِ اللهِ الصَّالِحِينَ. أَلسَّلاَمُ عَلَيْكُمْ وَ رَحْمَةُ اللهِ وَ بَرَكَاتُهُ.

↓

Second *Rak'at* - Three Recommended *Takbīrs* to "conclude" the *Ṣalāt*[46]	
	أَللهُ أَكْبَرُ. أَللهُ أَكْبَرُ. أَللهُ أَكْبَرُ.

A Short Window of Opportunity

One of the thought-provoking aspects of Ṣalāt al-Ghufaylah is the fact that the time window in which this ṣalāt needs to be performed is quite short, and when we look at all the other obligatory and recommended prayers, we see that we have the shortest time available to perform this specific one.

---

46 In the teachings of the Ahlul Bayt ﷺ, the *ṣalāt* is completed with the recitation of the *salām* - however it is highly recommended to finalize the *ṣalāt* with three *takbīrs*, then continue the recitation of the *taʿqibāt* of the *ṣalāt*.

Scholars state that the actual time for Ṣalāt al-Ghufaylah begins right after the completion of Ṣalāt al-Maghrib (when prayed as time sets in) and the time for its "ends" when the redness from the sun completely leaves the western sky.

Therefore, if a person recites the *adhān* and *iqāmah* and then performs *Ṣalāt al-Maghrib* right when the time sets in and then continues with the minimum *ta'qibāt* - such as the *tasbīḥ* of Fāṭima al-Zahrā 🌹, and if all of this takes around 15 minutes, then one will have approximately 10 minutes to complete the entire performance of *Ṣalāt al-Ghufaylah*.

It is possible that the time is so short in performing this prayer because it is one in which a believer is seeking one's salvation and in such a precarious situation, naturally the time is limited to save oneself. If a believer delays in saving oneself, then one will naturally fall into complete darkness and disarray, and therefore one must ensure that one strives to perform this prayer during its limited and specific time frame.

However, we should note that if one does not have the opportunity to perform it at its specified time, this does not mean that one should not perform it at all! If one performs this *ṣalāt* between *Maghrib* and *'Ishā'*, they will, without a doubt, receive its reward and even if one was to delay in its performance, they would still be granted a share of the rewards.[47] In addition, if one was not able to perform it between *Maghrib* and *'Ishā'* they are also advised to perform it after *'Ishā'* for attaining its rewards and blessings.

The Dhikr Yūnusiyyah

As with all acts of worship, we know that they are not just movements to perform and check off the list of being "done"; rather

---

[47] Based on the reply from the office of Āyatullāh al-Uẓmā al-Ḥājj al-Sayyid 'Alī al-Ḥusaynī al-Sīstānī via www.najaf.org on July 4, 2016.

they are means to a higher goal - spiritual proximity to Allah ﷻ and to earn His pleasure. Such an ambitious objective cannot be reached if we do not understand what we are doing and why we are doing it. Allah ﷻ tells us in the Qurān:

﴿يَا أَيُّهَا الَّذِينَ آمَنُوا لَا تَقْرَبُوا الصَّلَاةَ وَأَنتُمْ سُكَارَىٰ حَتَّىٰ تَعْلَمُوا مَا تَقُولُونَ ﴿٤٣﴾﴾

> O you who have faith! Do not approach prayer when you are intoxicated, [not] until you know what you are saying...[48]

One of the interpretations given for not praying while 'intoxicated until we know what we are saying' is to ensure that not only are we fully awake, but also that we are aware and understand what we are saying, and this knowledge of what is being said and done cannot be fully appreciated until we comprehend the meanings behind what is being recited.

Perhaps one of the proofs for why the performance of *Ṣalāt al-Ghufaylah* has been recommended and why grand rewards have been mentioned for it is because in it, the *Dhikr Yūnusiyyah* - the prayer of Prophet Yūnus ibn Mittai ﷺ - has been mentioned. It was this Prophet who, for one brief instance, fell into a state of heedlessness and separated away from his community and in the end, his outcome was that he was put into the tumultuous waters, and eventually ended up in the belly of a massive fish. It was only after his remorse towards Allah ﷻ, the Gracious, that he finally found salvation. Perhaps due to this life-changing event in his life, the Ahlul Bayt ﷺ have stated that due to the minor and major periods of spiritual negligence which we fall into daily, we should seek salvation from the outward and inward forms of spiritual

---

[48] Qurān, Sūrah al-Nisā' (4), verse 43.

gloom through remembering these poignant verses of the Glorious Qurān.

Prophet Yūnus ﷺ - A Prophet of Many "Exceptions"

Born around the year 825 BCE and buried in the northern Iraqi city of Mosul, Prophet Yūnus ﷺ was, by all accounts, a Prophet of many "exceptions". A masjid and burial site for this great Prophet of Allah ﷻ stood for thousands of years in this city until its destruction at the hands of "Daesh" (also known as ISIS/ISIL/IS) around July 25th, 2014.

Some historians have mentioned that he was a prophet from the Children of Israel and came after Prophet Sulaymān ﷺ to the people of Nineveh (Naynawā). He is spoken about in the Book of Jonah in the Old Testament of the Bible,[49] and has been mentioned on five occasions in the Noble Qurān.

In the fourth Sūrah of the Qurān, verse 163, he is mentioned alongside a host of Prophets who received revelations:

﴿إِنَّآ أَوۡحَيۡنَآ إِلَيۡكَ كَمَآ أَوۡحَيۡنَآ إِلَىٰ نُوحٖ وَٱلنَّبِيِّـۧنَ مِنۢ بَعۡدِهِۦۚ وَأَوۡحَيۡنَآ إِلَىٰٓ إِبۡرَٰهِيمَ وَإِسۡمَٰعِيلَ وَإِسۡحَٰقَ وَيَعۡقُوبَ وَٱلۡأَسۡبَاطِ وَعِيسَىٰ وَأَيُّوبَ وَيُونُسَ وَهَٰرُونَ وَسُلَيۡمَٰنَۚ وَءَاتَيۡنَا دَاوُۥدَ زَبُورٗا ١٦٣﴾

> We have indeed revealed to you (Muḥammad) as We revealed to Nūḥ and the Prophets after him, and [as] We revealed to Ibrāhīm and Ismāʿīl and Isḥāq and Yaʿqūb and the Tribes and ʿIsā and Ayyūb and **Yūnus** and Hārūn and Sulaymān, and We gave Dāwūd the Psalms.[50]

In Sūrah 6, verses 84 to 87, he is referred to alongside other Prophets as being 'rightly-guided':

---

[49] The passage in reference has been quoted at the end of this book in Appendix III.

[50] Qurān, Sūrah al-Nisā' (4), verse 163.

﴿وَوَهَبْنَا لَهُۥٓ إِسْحَٰقَ وَيَعْقُوبَ ۚ كُلًّا هَدَيْنَا ۚ وَنُوحًا هَدَيْنَا مِن قَبْلُ ۖ وَمِن
ذُرِّيَّتِهِۦ دَاوُۥدَ وَسُلَيْمَٰنَ وَأَيُّوبَ وَيُوسُفَ وَمُوسَىٰ وَهَٰرُونَ ۚ وَكَذَٰلِكَ
نَجْزِى ٱلْمُحْسِنِينَ ﴿٨٤﴾ وَزَكَرِيَّا وَيَحْيَىٰ وَعِيسَىٰ وَإِلْيَاسَ ۖ كُلٌّ مِّنَ
ٱلصَّٰلِحِينَ ﴿٨٥﴾ وَإِسْمَٰعِيلَ وَٱلْيَسَعَ وَيُونُسَ وَلُوطًا ۚ وَكُلًّا فَضَّلْنَا عَلَى
ٱلْعَٰلَمِينَ ﴿٨٦﴾ وَمِنْ ءَابَآئِهِمْ وَذُرِّيَّٰتِهِمْ وَإِخْوَٰنِهِمْ ۖ وَٱجْتَبَيْنَٰهُمْ وَهَدَيْنَٰهُمْ
إِلَىٰ صِرَٰطٍ مُّسْتَقِيمٍ ﴿٨٧﴾﴾

And We gave him Isḥāq and Yaʿqūb and We guided each one of them. And Nūḥ We had guided before, and from his offspring, Dāwūd and Sulaymān and Ayyūb and Yūsuf and Mūsā and Hārūn - and thus do We reward the virtuous; and Zakariyyā and Yaḥyā and ʿIsā and Ilyās - each of them among the righteous; and Ismāʿīl and Yasaʿa and **Yūnus** and Lūṭ - each We graced over all of the nations; and from among their fathers, their descendants and their brethren - We chose them and guided them to a Straight Path.[51]

From a verse in the Qurān in Sūrah 10, verse 98, it seems that Prophet Yūnus's ﷺ community was the only one who was spared the Divine retribution due to their repentance:

﴿فَلَوْلَا كَانَتْ قَرْيَةٌ آمَنَتْ فَنَفَعَهَا إِيمَانُهَا إِلَّا قَوْمَ يُونُسَ لَمَّا آمَنُوا
كَشَفْنَا عَنْهُمْ عَذَابَ الْخِزْيِ فِي الْحَيَاةِ الدُّنْيَا وَمَتَّعْنَاهُمْ إِلَىٰ
حِينٍ ﴿٩٨﴾﴾

Why has there not been any town that might believe, so that its belief might benefit it, except the people of **Yūnus**? When they believed, We removed from them the punishment of

[51] Qurān, Sūrah al-Anʿām (6), verses 84-87.

> disgrace in the life of this world, and We provided to them for a while.[52]

The last mention of him in the Qurān reads as follows:

﴿وَإِنَّ يُونُسَ لَمِنَ الْمُرْسَلِينَ ﴿١٣٩﴾ إِذْ أَبَقَ إِلَى الْفُلْكِ الْمَشْحُونِ ﴿١٤٠﴾
فَسَاهَمَ فَكَانَ مِنَ الْمُدْحَضِينَ ﴿١٤١﴾ فَالْتَقَمَهُ الْحُوتُ وَهُوَ مُلِيمٌ ﴿١٤٢﴾
فَلَوْلَا أَنَّهُ كَانَ مِنَ الْمُسَبِّحِينَ ﴿١٤٣﴾ لَلَبِثَ فِي بَطْنِهِ إِلَىٰ يَوْمِ يُبْعَثُونَ ﴿١٤٤﴾
فَنَبَذْنَاهُ بِالْعَرَاءِ وَهُوَ سَقِيمٌ ﴿١٤٥﴾ وَأَنْبَتْنَا عَلَيْهِ شَجَرَةً مِنْ يَقْطِينٍ ﴿١٤٦﴾
وَأَرْسَلْنَاهُ إِلَىٰ مِائَةِ أَلْفٍ أَوْ يَزِيدُونَ ﴿١٤٧﴾ فَآمَنُوا فَمَتَّعْنَاهُمْ إِلَىٰ حِينٍ
﴿١٤٨﴾﴾

> And indeed, **Yūnus** was one of the Messengers, when he fled toward the laden ship. Then he drew lots with them and he was the one to be refuted. Then the fish swallowed him while he was blameworthy. And had he not been one of those who praise God's glory, he would have surely remained in its belly until the day they will be resurrected. Then We cast him on a bare shore, and he was sick. So, We made a gourd plant grow above him. We sent him to a [community of] a hundred thousand or more, and they believed [in him]. So, We provided for them for a while.[53]

Amongst all the Prophets mentioned in the Qurān, Prophet Yūnus ﷷ is the only one who has many 'exceptions' within his life. Although all the Messengers of Allah ﷿ exemplified different traits, led unique lives, and had inimitable experiences, Prophet

[52] Qurān, Sūrah Yūnus (10), verse 98.
[53] Ibid., Sūrah al-Ṣaffāt (37), verses 139-148.

Yūnus ﷺ is seen as one of the 'exceptions' to all the Prophets which we have been told about for the following reasons:

1. He is perhaps the only Prophet who has been 'rebuked' by Allah ﷻ twice in his life. The first instance is seen in Sūrah al-Ṣāffāt, verses 143 and 144, in which we are told that if he had not been among those who praise Allah ﷻ, then he would have remained in the belly of the fish until the Day of Resurrection. In the second instance we read in Sūrah al-Qalam, verse 49, that if he had not experienced the Divine blessings from his Lord, then he would have been expelled onto a dry, deserted island. Scholars state that this shows that as two different penalties have been stated, he was reproached by Allah ﷻ on two separate occasions.

2. His people are also an 'exception' just as this Prophet was because they are the only community which we can find in the Qurān that were spared of the Divine punishment and were given another chance at servitude.

3. Another 'exception' which exists in the life of Prophet Yūnus ﷺ is that even though he has an entire Sūrah of the Qurān named after him, there is no mention of him in that chapter! When we look at other chapters of the Qurān, its name - in almost all cases - reflects a theme, topic or word found in that chapter; and when we reflect on the chapters named after Prophets or the inspirational men and women of the Qurān, they are always spoken about, and some aspect of their lives is covered in that chapter. However, looking at Sūrah Yūnus, there is just one reference in which his community has been mentioned - and that too, it speaks about them when he was not even among his community. It says:

﴿فَلَوْلَا كَانَتْ قَرْيَةٌ آمَنَتْ فَنَفَعَهَا إِيمَانُهَا إِلَّا قَوْمَ يُونُسَ لَمَّا آمَنُوا كَشَفْنَا عَنْهُمْ عَذَابَ الْخِزْيِ فِي الْحَيَاةِ الدُّنْيَا وَمَتَّعْنَاهُمْ إِلَىٰ حِينٍ ﴿٩٨﴾﴾

Why has there not been any town that might believe, so that its belief might benefit it, except the people of Yūnus? When they believed (after he had left them), We removed from them the punishment of disgrace in the life of this world, and We provided for them for a while.[54]

4. Another 'exception' which this Prophet had in his life is the form of 'punishment' which he was subjected to. Even though the prophets of Allah ﷻ which came before and after him all suffered untold horrors, none of them were ever subject to being thrown into the tumultuous waves and being swallowed by a large fish and spending time, imprisoned, in the belly of such a beast.

5. We also see that an approximate number of people who were a part of his community is expressly mentioned in the Qurān - something not seen for any other Prophet. Allah ﷻ tells us in Sūrah al-Ṣāffāt, verse 147 that:

﴿وَأَرْسَلْنَاهُ إِلَىٰ مِائَةِ أَلْفٍ أَوْ يَزِيدُونَ ﴿١٤٧﴾﴾

We sent him to a [community of] a hundred thousand or more...[55]

Even more than this is the fact that Allah ﷻ also tells us the number of people who believed in him - again, something not seen for any other Prophet in the Qurān, as we read in the verse which follows:

[54] Qurān, Sūrah Yūnus (10), verse 98.
[55] Ibid., Sūrah al-Ṣāffāt (37), verse 147.

﴿فَـَٔامَنُوا۟ ﴿١٤٨﴾﴾

...and they [the one-hundred-thousand people] believed [in him].[56]

Exegesis on the First Verse Recited in Ṣalāt al-Ghufaylah[57]

To better appreciate this *ṣalāt* and ensure that the spiritual powers of this prayer are completely realized, we need to fully understand the two verses of the Qurān which we recite in this prayer. Therefore, let us now delve into their commentary, as explained by the contemporary exegete of the Qurān, Āyatullāh al-Uẓmā Shaykh Nāṣir Makārim Shīrāzī, in his work, *Tafsīr Namuneh.*

﴿وَذَا ٱلنُّونِ إِذ ذَّهَبَ مُغَـٰضِبًا فَظَنَّ أَن لَّن نَّقْدِرَ عَلَيْهِ فَنَادَىٰ فِى ٱلظُّلُمَـٰتِ أَن لَّآ إِلَـٰهَ إِلَّآ أَنتَ سُبْحَـٰنَكَ إِنِّى كُنتُ مِنَ ٱلظَّـٰلِمِينَ ﴿٨٧﴾ فَٱسْتَجَبْنَا لَهُۥ وَنَجَّيْنَـٰهُ مِنَ ٱلْغَمِّ ۚ وَكَذَٰلِكَ نُـۨجِى ٱلْمُؤْمِنِينَ ﴿٨٨﴾﴾

And the Man of the Fish (Prophet Yūnus), when he left in a rage, thinking that We would not put him to hardship. Then he cried out in the darkness: 'There is no god except You! You are immaculate! I have indeed been among the wrongdoers!' So, We answered his prayer and delivered him from the agony; and thus, do We deliver the faithful ones.[58]

56 Quran, Sūrah al-Ṣāffāt (37), verse 148.

57 *Tafsīr Namuneh* of Āyatullāh al-Uẓmā Shaykh Nāṣir Makārim Shīrāzī, vol. 13, pp. 484 - 489.

58 Qurān, Sūrah al-Anbiyā' (21), verses 87 - 88.

Salvation of Prophet Yūnus ﵇ from the Frightful Agony

These two verses offer us a glimpse into the outcome of this great man of God, Prophet Yūnus ﵇ where we first read: 'And the Man of the Fish (Prophet Yūnus), when he left in a rage...'

The meaning of the word *nūn* (translated as fish) in this verse is a large fish - something such as a whale - and therefore the meaning of the phrase *dhā'n nūn* is literally "The Man of the Fish" and the choice of this name for Prophet Yūnus ﵇ is due to the event which we will soon relate.

The verse continues: '...thinking that We would not put him to hardship.'[59]

Prophet Yūnus ﵇ believed that he had fulfilled his responsibility of propagation towards his disobedient community and that his leaving the society would not even be considered as an act which is referred to as *tark al-awlā*[60] and that there was absolutely nothing wrong with him leaving his people in the state that they were in of disbelief and in turn, parting his region. However, what would have been "better" in this circumstance was that he should have stayed among them and displayed the best form of patience and fortitude, yearning that perhaps his community would spiritually awaken and make their way towards Allah ﷻ.

---

[59] The word *naqdiru* or 'hardship' comes from the root *qa-da-ra,* and it means to be strict or restraining, because anytime a person gets strict with someone or something, it means that at the same time, he is also constraining that person or thing and is not expanding nor taking account of things.

[60] Loosely defined, this is when a Prophet does something which is not befitting of a man of his status - but this is never considered as a sin or a transgression against the laws of Allāh ﷻ. Rather, it is the case of choosing something which is "not too good" over something which is "better." (Tr.)

In the end, it is due to this act of *tark al-awlā* which he performed that he fell into this predicament and found himself inside the belly of a mighty fish who ended up swallowing him alive; and while he was in the multiple layers of darkness, he made the passionate and famous prayer: 'Then he cried out in the darkness: 'There is no god except You! You are immaculate! I have indeed been among the wrongdoers!''

Through this supplication, Prophet Yūnus ﷺ testified that not only had he been unfair to his own self, but also to his community; had he continued to endure their attitude and bear a few more difficulties, the community may have joined his path.

Allah ﷻ then says: 'So We answered his prayer and delivered him from the agony; and thus, do We rescue the faithful ones.'

This supplication is not merely an agenda for change which was limited to Prophet Yūnus ﷺ, rather it is both a prayer and a state of mind which any individual who considers oneself to be a believer and finds that they have fallen short in their responsibilities should make and seek to enter into. Thus, every believer should ask Allah ﷻ to overlook one's lapses and shortcomings, and seek assistance and mercy from His pure essence, for surely Allah ﷻ has guaranteed that He will answer the supplications and alleviate the grief of anyone who turns towards Him sincerely.

Points of Reflection

The Outcome of Prophet Yūnus ﷺ

We will leave the detailed discussion of Prophet Yūnus ﷺ to the commentary of Sūrah al-Ṣaffāt,[61] however the summary of this discussion is what follows.

---

[61] We have translated this passage and have included it in this book as Appendix I.

Prophet Yūnus ﷺ spent many years with his community in Nineveh in present day ʿIrāq, busy inviting them to the true religion and propagating the correct faith. However, no matter how much he tried, his guidance fell on deaf ears, and because of this, he became infuriated and left them to go towards the sea.

When he reached his destination, he boarded a ship and set sail. In the middle of the journey, a huge storm began to form, creating large waves on the water; and within a short time, it became apparent to the ship's captain and all on board that if they did not do something soon, then everyone on the boat would perish.

The captain of the ship said: "I think that from among you all, there is a run-away slave who needs to be thrown into the sea (to remove this curse from us)." Other reports mention that he may have stated: "The boat has become too heavy with so many people on it, and thus we need to remove one person - we will determine who this is by drawing lots." They drew lots of numerous times and every time, the name of Prophet Yūnus ﷺ came up and from this the Prophet understood that a hidden message [from Allah ﷻ] was being conveyed to him. He promptly submitted to the outcome and jumped off the ship. When he landed into the water, a large fish swallowed him up - however, Allah ﷻ allowed him to remain alive in the belly of the fish through a miracle.

Eventually, Prophet Yūnus ﷺ realized that he had performed an act which was deemed as a *tark al-awlā* and he turned back towards Allah ﷻ in repentance and submitted to his culpability; and because of this, Allah ﷻ accepted his supplication and saved him from the belly of the fish.[62]

It is possible that some people may consider this event as something which is not scientifically possible and state that this was carried out through an act which defies the normal laws of the world. Although it may not be something logical, all other acts of

---

[62] *Tafsīr al-Kabīr*; *Tafsīr Majmaʿ al-Bayān*; *Tafsīr Nūr al-Thaqalayn*, under the verse of discussion.

the prophets of Allah ﷻ are similar – for example, the dead being brought back to life by Prophet ʿIsā ؑ, or the parting of the sea by Prophet Mūsā ؑ, and other such miracles by various saints of Allah ﷻ (all such things are possible by His permission.) Therefore, what occurred to Prophet Yūnus ؑ in this story is also considered to be something out of the ordinary, however it is not something which is outside of the intellect as being possible. In other words, such actions are not possible to be done under normal circumstances; but with help from the universal power of the Sustainer, it is probable and possible. For more details on this event, please refer to the commentary found in Sūrah al-Ṣāffāt [found in Appendix I].

What is the Meaning of "Darkness" in this Passage?

This phrase may refer to the collective darkness of the sea, the depths of the water, the darkness experienced in the belly of the fish, and the darkness of the night. We have a tradition from Imām Muḥammad al-Bāqir ؑ which states:

لَبِثَ يُونُسَ فِي بَطْنِ الْحُوتِ ثَلاَثَةَ أَيَّامٍ، وَ نَادٰى فِي الظُّلُمَاتِ ظُلْمَةِ
بَطْنِ الْحُوتِ، وَ ظُلْمَةِ اللَّيْلِ، وَ ظُلْمَةِ الْبَحْرِ: أَنْ لاَ إِلٰهَ إِلَّا أَنْتَ سُبْحَانَكَ
إِنِّي كُنْتُ مِنَ الظَّالِمِينَ فَاسْتَجَابَ لَهُ - رَبُّهُ

> Yūnus remained in the stomach of the fish for three days and he called out from the darknesses: the darkness of the stomach of the fish, the darkness of the night, and the darkness of the waters that, "There is no god except You! You are immaculate! I have indeed been among the wrongdoers!" and therefore, His Lord answered his prayer.[63]

[63] *Tafsīr Nūr al-Thaqalayn*, vol. 3, pg. 450.

What is the *Tark al-Awlā* that Prophet Yūnus ﷷ Performed?

Undeniably, the term *mughāḍhiban* or "when he (Yūnus ﷷ) left in a state of rage" refers to the anger which Prophet Yūnus ﷷ exhibited towards the unbelieving people of his community. Such a form of anger and disappointment, in these instances in which a Prophet of Allah ﷻ spends countless years in trying to guide his erroneous community but in response to his good-willed intention of guiding them they refuse to accept it, is something which is completely natural.

From another angle, Prophet Yūnus ﷷ knew that the punishment of Allah ﷻ would shortly come down upon his people, and thus him leaving the city or village was not considered as a sin; however for a great Prophet such as Yūnus ﷷ, it would have better that he stayed with them until the last minute, just before the punishment of Allah ﷻ descended upon them and not to leave them alone; or [that he should have waited for the specific time] when Allah ﷻ commanded him to leave. It is for this reason that his haste was considered as a *tark al-awlā*, and Prophet Yūnus ﷷ was held culpable by Allah ﷻ. This is the same understanding which can be gleamed from the story of Prophet Ādam ﷷ in which it was stated that such actions are not considered as an <u>absolute sin</u>, but rather they are considered as <u>relative offenses</u>; or to employ another phrase, we can state that they are an epitome of the understanding:

حَسَنَاتُ الأَبْرَارِ سَيِّئَاتُ الْمُقَرَّبِينَ

Good deeds of the righteous ones are considered as sins for those in proximity (to Allah).[64]

---

[64] For further details, refer to volume six of *Tafsīr Namuneh*, page 122.

A Fateful Lesson Learnt

The very meaningful portion of this verse which reads: '...and thus do We deliver the faithful ones' clearly shows us that whatever happened to Prophet Yūnus 🙿 - both the challenge he found himself in and his deliverance and salvation - is not something which is specifically limited to him. Rather, by preserving the hierarchy of the event and everything which transpired within it, we understand that this is something which affects everyone equally.

Many of the grief-initiating events, heart-rending life trials, and difficult tribulations which we encounter on a day-to-day basis are brought about through our own sins. These are metaphorical lashings which are inflicted upon us to awaken our spiritually asleep souls, or sometimes they are like a high temperature furnace which is used to cleanse metal from its impurities. Any time an individual finds oneself in such a situation, one should sit back and reflect on the following three points which Prophet Yūnus 🙿 found himself in, then one can rectify one's own actions and realize that salvation will come:

1. Paying close attention to the reality of *Tawḥīd* and that there is not a single creation, nor any anchor which can be relied upon other than Allah ﷻ.
2. One must consider Allah ﷻ to be free from all sorts of defects and deficiencies, and that He does not commit any act of oppression against His servants, and one must never have a bad estimation of Allah ﷻ.
3. One must confess one's sins only to Allah ﷻ and not to anyone else and seek His forgiveness.

These points can be better understood in the light of a tradition mentioned in the exegesis of the Noble Qurān, *Durr al-Manthūr* which has been narrated from the Prophet of Islām 🙿 where he said:

إِسْمُ اللهِ الَّذِي إِذَا دُعِيَ بِهِ أَجَابَ وَ إِذَا سُئِلَ بِهِ أَعْطَى دَعَوْتَ يُونُسَ بْنُ مَتَّى. قِيلَ: يَا رَسُولَ اللهِ هِيَ لِيُونُسَ خَاصَّةً أَمْ لِجَمَاعَةِ الْمُسْلِمِينَ؟ قَالَ: هِيَ لِيُونُسَ خَاصَّةً وَ لِلْمُؤْمِنَيْنِ إِذَا دُعُوا بِهَا أَ لَمْ تَسْمَعْ قَوْلَ اللهِ: ﴿وَ كَذٰلِكَ نُنْجِي الْمُؤْمِنِينَ﴾ فَهُوَ شَرْطٍ مِنَ اللهُ لِمَنْ دَعَاهُ

> One of the names of Allah which if anyone calls upon Him through it, will be given a response; and which if anyone requests anything from Him through it, will be granted one's wish is the 'dhikr of Yūnus, the son of Mattā'." A person said: 'O Messenger of Allah! Was that *(dhikr)* restricted solely to [Prophet] Yūnus or does it include all the believing Muslims [meaning can we also recite it and be granted by Allah]?!' The Prophet replied: 'It is both for Yūnus, and for all the believers when they call upon Him (Allah) with that same recitation. Have you not read what Allah says in the Qurān: '...and thus do We grant deliverance to the believers'? This is proof that anyone who calls upon Allah with this supplication, Allah will answer that person, for surely He has guaranteed this!'[65]

It goes without saying that this grand blessing of having anything granted to an individual does not mean that we simply 'recite' this passage, rather we must seek to practically implement its universal message within ourselves - meaning that in addition to its verbal declaration, our entire presence and essence must resonate with this supplication and its meaning in every stage of our lives.

It is vital for us to understand that the retributions of Allah ﷻ are of two types:

---

65 *Tafsīr Durr al-Manthūr*, as narrated in *Al-Mizān fi Tasfīr al-Qurān* under the verse in discussion.

1. The first is considered as a 'concluding punishment' which results in a person's complete breakdown, and which cannot be atoned for and as such, there is no supplication available which will benefit a person who is about to suffer this form of punishment. This is the case where before such a chastisement is warranted for an individual, the above-mentioned program [of warnings] is repeated, and as such, an individual is given numerous chances to rectify oneself.
2. The second type is a 'punitive punishment' which has an aspect of spiritual training for the individual in it. In this instance, since the punishment is merely to internally awaken the individual and acquaint a person with one's negative actions, this category of retribution is also quick to be rescinded from a person if the individual fulfills all the prerequisites.

From these points of discussion, it becomes clear that the philosophy of tribulations and misfortunes, and other such upheavals which people go through in life is to spiritually awaken them and aide in their spiritual teaching and coaching.

Not only do the events which Prophet Yūnus ﷺ experienced in different areas offer warnings to all of the leaders who guide people towards the truth that they should never think that the propagation of the message which they are charged with will ever come to an end, they must also never consider their struggles in this path as being insignificant, for such individuals carry a weighty responsibility upon their shoulders.

Lessons to Learn from the First Verse Recited in Ṣalāt al-Ghufaylah[66]

1. When conveying historical events, we should not only stick to relating the pleasant and successful events which transpired -

[66] Extracted from *Tafsīr Nūr* of Shaykh Muḥsin Qarā'atī.

we must balance it by also speaking about the bitter and failed experiences.

2. We must never feel that our Divinely ordained responsibility of conveying His message has ended, thus ever abandoning it.
3. Sometimes an action done in haste and without proper consideration and permission will result in retribution.
4. Allah ﷻ is All-Knowledgeable about our thoughts, opinions, and notions.
5. There are times when the Prophets of Allah ؑ are not given access to the knowledge of what will transpire in the future.
6. One display of unwarranted anger can lead even a Prophet of Allah ؑ into a precarious situation in his life.
7. There are times when an unjustified action can lead a person to go through several types of spiritual darknesses.
8. When going forth to analyze tribulations that we go through in life, we must always remember that Allah ﷻ is blameless and innocent and realize that we need to delve deep into our own actions to see where the problem lies.
9. In all our actions, if our expressions of love and hate are not based on the orders of Allah ﷻ and seeking His pleasure, then we will not reach a successful outcome in our lives.
10. Confessing one's sins solely in the presence of Allah ﷻ is one form of perfection and is one of the etiquettes of supplication *(dūʿāʾ)*.
11. Those supplications which contain the professing of the Oneness of Allah *(Tawḥīd)*, expressing the immaculate nature of Allah ﷻ and confessing one's mistakes, slips and sins are supplications which will be answered and accepted.
12. The transcendence of Allah ﷻ and our testifying to our sins is the secret of our salvation from self-inflicted spiritual afflictions and to acquire those things which we may have otherwise been prevented from attaining.

13. The only path towards salvation is through the will and intention of Allah ﷻ.
14. The stories of the Qurān are events which have no end to them - they are timeless - and present to us a perpetual custom *(sunnah).*
15. The salvation granted to the people of true faith *(īmān)* is a custom *(sunnah)* and a universal legislation of Allah ﷻ.
16. Whoever recites this recitation *(dhikr)* of Prophet Yūnus ﷺ will be guaranteed salvation.

Exegesis on the Second Verse Recited in Ṣalāt al-Ghufaylah[67]

﴿وَعِندَهُۥ مَفَاتِحُ ٱلۡغَيۡبِ لَا يَعۡلَمُهَآ إِلَّا هُوَۚ وَيَعۡلَمُ مَا فِي ٱلۡبَرِّ وَٱلۡبَحۡرِۚ وَمَا تَسۡقُطُ مِن وَرَقَةٍ إِلَّا يَعۡلَمُهَا وَلَا حَبَّةٖ فِي ظُلُمَٰتِ ٱلۡأَرۡضِ وَلَا رَطۡبٖ وَلَا يَابِسٍ إِلَّا فِي كِتَٰبٖ مُّبِينٖ ٥٩﴾

And with Him are the treasures of the Unseen; no one knows them except for Him. He knows whatever there is in the land and the sea. No leaf falls without His knowing it, nor is there a grain in the darkness of the earth, nor anything fresh or withered but it is in a manifest Book.[68]

Knowledge of the Unseen (ʿIlm al-Ghayb)

In other verses of the Quran, there is talk about the Knowledge and Power of Allah ﷻ, and the vastness of the domain of His commands - and what is discussed in this verse, which was mentioned only in brief in other places of the Quran, is further elucidated upon here.

---

[67] *Tafsīr Namuneh*, vol. 5, pp. 268 - 272.

[68] Qurān, Sūrah al-Anʿām (6), verse 59.

The first sphere of discussion is regarding the Knowledge of Allah ﷻ where it says: 'And with Him are the treasures of the Unseen; no one knows them except for Him.'

The word *mafātiḥ* - meaning "keys" - is the plural of *miftaḥ*[69] which means "key" and it is also possible that this word is the plural of *maftaḥ*[70] which means "treasury" or "the place where valuable things are kept."

In the first instance, the verse would mean that "all of the **keys** of the unseen are in His hands;" while in the second instance, the verse would mean that "all of the **treasures** of the unseen are with Him."

Another possibility also exists which states that both meanings are intended in this passage, just as we have proven in the Science of Islamic Jurisprudence *('Ilm al-Uṣūl)* that the usage of one phrase for multiple meanings is not a problem and, in both instances, these two meanings are dependent on one another. Often when there is treasure, it is necessary that there should also be a key (to safeguard it by having that treasure locked in a safe).

However, it is better to state that *mafātiḥ* used in the verse means "keys" and not a "treasury" as the goal of this verse is to expound upon the depths of the Knowledge of Allah ﷻ, and that is connected to 'keys' which are the means through which one gains an understanding of the various hidden mysteries.

It should be mentioned that in the two other instances in which the word *mafātiḥ* has been used in the Qurān, the meaning of the word there is also "keys."[71]

---

[69] Note the *kasrah* on the first letter. (Tr)

[70] Note the *fatha* on the first letter. (Tr)

[71] Other usages of this word in the Qurān occur in Sūrah al-Qaṣaṣ (26), verse 76:

﴿أَنتُمْ وَءَابَآؤُكُمُ ٱلْأَقْدَمُونَ ﴿٧٦﴾﴾

"...that their **keys** indeed proved heavy for a band of proponents."

To further elucidate upon and add emphasis to the extent of His knowledge, we read: 'He knows whatever there is in the land and the sea.'

The word *barr* - "land" means 'an expansive area' and is usually used for 'dry land;' while the original meaning of the word *baḥr* - "sea" also means 'an expansive area,' however one which 'a large body of water covers over;' and usually rivers or sometimes even large streams are referred to with this word in ʿArabic.

Therefore, the Knowledge of Allah ﷻ encompasses everything on the land and that which is in the seas - meaning that His knowledge basically encompasses everything in existence.

By keeping in mind the capacious meaning of this portion of the verse: 'He knows whatever there is in the land and the sea' this actually clarifies to us the expanse of His Knowledge. By this, we mean that He has Knowledge of the millions of creations in existence; the smallest to the largest - whether they exist in the depths of the waters or on the land, such as the leaves on the trees which are in the forests, jungles and mountains; it includes the history of each bud of a blossom and every flower which blooms; it includes the gusts of wind over the land and those which move across the desert; it includes the number of cells in the body of each and every single human being and even the quantity of blood cells in each person; it includes the enigmatic movements of every single electron within the deep recesses of each atom; and ultimately it includes even the passing thoughts of each and every individual in existence and all of those which even impact upon the depths of our souls. Yes indeed, His knowledge equally covers these and many other areas!

This word is also used in Sūrah al-Nūr (24), verse 61:

﴿...أَوْ مَا مَلَكْتُم مَّفَاتِحَهُۥٓ...﴾

"...or those whose **keys** are in your possession..."

In the next sentence, to further emphasize the comprehensive knowledge of Allah ﷻ, we are directed towards a specific instance of His knowledge where He says: 'No leaf falls without His knowing it...'

From this, we understand that the total number of these leaves and the precise instance in which they separate from the branches which they were once a part of, and their spinning in the air as they make their way to the ground until they finally touch down, are all within the realm of His infinite Knowledge.

The verse continues: '…nor is there a grain in the darkness of the earth…' except that all its specifics are also within Allah's Knowledge. In this portion of the verse, we can place our finger on two very precise and distinctive areas which no human being - even if they were to live millions of years and were to develop the most complete, amazing pieces of technology - would ever be able to grasp.

Who knows which seeds have been separated by the winds from the innumerable plants, which blow day and night around this planet, and where they will eventually settle down? Indeed, these could be seeds which may remain hidden deep within the recesses of the earth for many years, waiting for enough water be able to grow. Who knows how many seeds and from what kind of plants and on what point on this earth, in every hour of the day, are laid into this earth either by wild beasts or human beings walking around? Which electronic gadget can count the number of leaves which fall from the trees in the deepest, darkest forests and jungles of the world? Just looking at one forest, especially in the fall season and that too after a heavy rain or a strong wind and the scene of the leaves which have fallen, will verify this reality and from all of this, we acknowledge that it is not possible for any human being to have access to such levels of knowledge!

The exact instance of a leaf falling from a tree is its actual 'death,' while the dropping of the seeds into the deep depressions of the earth is that seed's first stage in being brought into life, and it is only Allah ﷻ who is fully aware of all these things within the system of life and death. Even the various stages of growth and progression which each grain goes through in its life towards perfection and maturing; only He is aware of that seed.

By Allah ﷻ bringing up this discussion, there are two effects of it - one is a philosophical outcome; and the other relates to the aspect of nurturing and the objective of human development.

As for the philosophical effect, it removes the erroneous belief from a person's mind that the Knowledge of Allah ﷻ is strictly limited to universals, and that Allah ﷻ does not have the knowledge of particulars - meaning the details of issues which occur in the world - but this clearly tells us that He has complete knowledge of both the particulars and the universals. As for the human developmental and nurturing aspect, the belief in such a comprehensive knowledge of Allah ﷻ communicates to the human being that despite all their hidden secrets, discourses, and even intentions and thoughts which run through one's mind - all of these are obvious and evident to Allah ﷻ. When such an acceptance becomes firmly rooted in an individual, then how is it possible that one does not try to watch over oneself and ensure that one has strict control over one's actions, words, and thoughts!?

At the end of this verse, we read: '...nor anything fresh or withered, but it is in a manifest Book.' Through a very short passage, this sentence presents the expansive and never-ending Knowledge of Allah ﷻ over all of creation and communicates to us that there is **nothing** which is hidden from His Knowledge.

The meaning of the words "fresh" and "withered" in this verse are not limited to their lexical definition - rather these words are used in their universal meaning.

The commentators of the Qurān have offered various possibilities for what the phrase "Manifest Book" *(Kitāb-i Mubīn)* means, however most of them state that this refers to the actual

Knowledge of Allah ﷻ - meaning that He encompasses knowledge regarding all His creations. It is also possible to say that the meaning of this is the "Preserved Tablet" *(Lawḥ al-Maḥfūẓ)* as it is probable that this is also a reference to the Knowledge of Allah ﷻ. Another probability exists which is that the meaning of the "Manifest Book" is the "World of Creation" and the continuous chain of cause and effect, and that all things are 'written' within that never-ending chain.

In other traditions which have been narrated from the Ahlul Bayt ﷺ the meaning of *waraqa* or 'leaf' are given of a fetus which has been aborted; the *ḥabbah* or 'seed' refers to a child; the phrase *ḍhulumāt al-arḍh* or 'in the darkness of the earth' refers to a mother's womb; the word *raṭb* or 'wet' refers to something wet; and *yābis* or 'dry' means something arid. Therefore, in explaining the reality of the verse in this way, the infallible Imāms from the family of the Prophet ﷺ wanted the Muslims to realize that they need to look at the verses of the Qurān with a broad scope and not limit themselves with merely the lexical definitions of the words. Rather, whenever there is an indication that there can be a wide-ranging meaning to a verse, then one must look to analyze and understand each verse in an expansive fashion.

Thus, the above-mentioned tradition points to the fact that the meaning of the verse under discussion is not strictly limited to the seeds of vegetables and other crops - rather, it can and does refer to the seeds of human life and existence as well.

Lessons to Learn from the Second Verse Recited in Ṣalāt al-Ghufaylah[72]

1. Although the disbelievers used to request that if God exists, that they wanted the Prophets to ask Him to hasten His punishment upon them, however as we know, this would not come about – as this is something reserved for Allāh ﷻ to

[72] Extracted from *Tafsīr-e Nūr.*

determine when He wishes to send down punishment and is within the Knowledge of the Unseen.

2. The rulings *(aḥkām)* which the Divine implements are based on His knowledge which covers the unseen and seen realms.
3. The scope of the knowledge of the unseen is much wider than normal forms of knowledge, and it is for this reason that the Qurān refers to it with specific phrases.
4. Contrary to what people may say that only Allah ﷻ Himself possesses a general knowledge of everything, we see in the Qurān that Allah's ﷻ knowledge spans over everything and encompasses particulars of the world of creation, and thus we need to be extra careful of each action that we perform.
5. Other than Allah ﷻ, none of the creations have access to the knowledge of the unseen realm [without His permission].
6. In the world, there is a central repository for all knowledge.
7. The world of creation has been created according to a pre-formulated plan.

Importance of Qunūt in the Daily Prayers

The word *qunūt* is derived from the Arabic root letters *qa-na-wa* and its lexical meaning is "to attain something by one's hands (working);" it can also mean "a ripened bunch of dates." However, in the Islamic terminology, its meaning is "obedience and worship coupled with humility and unpretentiousness" and thus its meaning within the Islamic terminology is to attain humbleness in worship through the acts within the prayer including the standing (for the recitation of the two chapters of the Qurān), genuflexion *(rukūʿ)*, and prostration *(sajdah)*. Of course, in the definition which the jurists offer for this word in the realm of Islamic jurisprudence, this word refers to a specific form of asking one's supplication *(dūʿāʾ)* in the presence of Allah ﷻ - but in a specific posture during the *ṣalāt* which has been prescribed as the lifting of one's hands with the palms facing the sky in front of one's face - ideally being placed parallel to one's nose.

The beauty of the *qunūt* lies in the fact that a person offering one's prayers - whether the obligatory or the recommended - is permitted at this juncture to make their requests and entreats known to Allah ﷻ in their own words and in their own language[73] - whether they be prayers for good in this world or for the next.

As for the *qunūt* in *Ṣalāt al-Ghufaylah*, it is truly a beautiful supplication which we make to Allah ﷻ. We begin by testifying to the ultimate power and knowledge of Allah ﷻ that He is aware of everything, and thus we are confirming the fact that we are about to ask for things which may not entirely be good for us to possess.

Since Allah ﷻ knows the unseen and seen, whereas we are limited to only the knowledge of the seen [and that too based on our extremely constrained scope of understanding], there are times in which we may desire things from this temporary, transient world which are not entirely good for us. Sometimes people desire enormous amounts of wealth, or certain types of knowledge, or to gain a spouse who has certain qualities and characteristics, or to

---

[73] Some scholars deem that in the obligatory daily prayers, only supplications in ʿArabic are permitted, while others permit supplications in *qunūt* to be performed in any language.

1. Āyatullāh al-ʿUẓmā Sayyid ʿAlī Ḥusaynī Sīstānī, Āyatullāh al-ʿUẓmā Shaykh Nāṣir Makārim al-Shīrāzī, Āyatullāh al-ʿUẓmā Shaykh Wahīd al-Khorasānī, and the late Āyatullāh al-ʿUẓmā Shaykh Luṭfullāh Ṣāfī al-Gulpāygānī state that: "One's prayer are correct, however they have not entirely fulfilled the prescription of performance of *qunūt* by reciting it in a language other than ʿArabic."

2. Āyatullāh al-ʿUẓmā Sayyid ʿAlī Ḥusaynī al-Khāmeneʾī states that: "According to precaution (obligatory precaution) one must recite the supplication of *qunūt* in ʿArabic, however one can refer to the next most knowledgeable scholar who has a ruling on this."

be blessed with copious children; but there is a strong possibility that what may seem "good" for us (in this life and the next) may not necessarily be so for us, or we may not be able to successfully manage and handle such things. It is for this reason that we remind ourselves in the *qunūt* of *ṣalāt al-ghufaylah* BEFORE we make our own appeals to Allah in our own words and language that only **HE** knows the unseen world and that He should grant us based on this.

As is a common practice and habit in the teachings of the Ahlul Bayt ﷩, before we make the request, we ask Allah ﷻ to first send His blessings upon Muḥammad ﷺ and the immaculate family of Muḥammad ﷩. Taking their names as intercessors and intermediaries is the essence of Monotheism *(Tawḥīd)* as we recognize that they are merely creations of Allah ﷻ - albeit the best of creations - but they can intercede for us by His permission.

We are then permitted to make our own prayers which are already known to Allah ﷻ - but this is where we need to consciously think about what it is that we want to ask from Allah ﷻ. We need to ensure that our requests are legitimate, "possible" and are things which will benefit us - not only in this life, but more so in the next world. We should always keep in mind the less fortunate people of our society, our immediate family members, friends, neighbours, and community members, and should then beseech Allah ﷻ for our own personal needs.

We close the *qunūt* in *Ṣalāt al-Ghufaylah* through a poignant supplication in which we once again turn our focus to the everlasting power and authority of Allah ﷻ and confirm that there is no one other than Him who can grant our requests and this includes friends, family, colleagues at work or anyone else - and that He alone is the source of grace and bounty for all of us. We testify to the fact that He has the power to respond to our requests, and that even if we do not verbally utter our needs, He still knows what is in our hearts; however, the *ḥadīth* tells us that Allah ﷻ

"likes" to hear His servant call out to Him and ask Him for one's needs - even if it be as "little" as shoelaces or a pinch of salt!

To complete the etiquette of *du'ā'*, we then end the *qunūt* by asking Allah 🕮 to once again send His blessings upon Muḥammad 🕮 and his family 🕮, and that all of our needs are granted just as we have been told that we should begin and end all of our supplications by asking for Divine grace to be bestowed upon the best of creations - Muḥammad 🕮 - and his noble family, the Ahlul Bayt 🕮.

The believer concludes one's *ṣalāt* in the normal process with confidence in one's heart that Allah 🕮 has heard the supplications that were asked, and that if what we have asked for is good for us in this world and in the next then He will grant it to us; but if there is any danger or harm to one's faith or conviction, then He delay that goodness and store the rewards of it for the next world.

As the recommended prayers are one of the ways which help a believer in one's spiritual ascent to Allah 🕮, and we have seen how the time between *Maghrib* and *'Ishā'* is one of the most important for such acts of worship, we present two other recommended prayers which can be performed within this time frame for those who wish to go above and beyond the 'minimal' spiritual regiment.

First Recommended Prayer between Maghrib and 'Ishā'

Other than this specific form of *Ṣalāt al-Ghufaylah* which has been discussed, we have been encouraged to recite other prayers between *Maghrib* and *'Ishā'* as well - specifically one which Prophet Muḥammad 🕮, while on his death bed, recommended Imām 'Alī 🕮 to perform.

It has been narrated in the traditions that when the Prophet 🕮 was about to pass away, Imām 'Alī 🕮 asked him to give him some advice, to which the Prophet replied:

أُوصِيكُمْ بِرَكْعَتَيْنِ بَيْنَ الْمَغْرِبِ وَالْعِشَاءِ الآخِرَةِ. تَقْرَءُ فِي الأُولىٰ اَلْحَمْدَ وَإِذَا زُلْزِلَتِ الأَرْضُ زِلْزَالَهَا ثَلاَثَ عَشَرَةَ مَرَّةً، وَالثَّانِيَةِ اَلْحَمْدَ وَقُلْ هُوَ اللّٰهُ أَحَدٌ خَمْسِينَ عَشَرَةَ مَرَّةً، فَإِنَّهُ مَنْ فَعَلَ ذٰلِكَ فِي كُلِّ شَهْرٍ، كَانَ مِنَ الْمُتَّقِينَ، فَإِنْ فَعَلَ ذٰلِكَ فِي كُلِّ سَنَةٍ كُتِبَ مِنَ الْمُحْسِنِينَ، فَإِنْ فَعَلَ فِي كُلِّ جُمْعَةٍ مَرَّةً كُتِبَ مِنَ الْمُصَلِّينَ، فَإِنْ فَعَلَ ذٰلِكَ فِي كُلِّ لَيْلَةٍ زَاحَمَنِي فِي الْجَنَّةِ وَلَمْ يَحْصَ ثَوَابَهُ إِلاَّ اللّٰهُ رَبُّ الْعَالَمِينَ جَلَّ وَ تَعَالَي

I advise you (all) to perform two *rakʿat* of prayers between *Maghrib* and *ʿIshāʾ* - in the first *rakʿat*, recite [Sūrah] al-Ḥamd (once), followed by [Sūrah] al-Zilzāl thirteen times; and in the second [*rakʿat*] recite [Sūrah] al-Ḥamd (once) followed by [Sūrah] al-Ikhlāṣ fifty times; and anyone who does this once a month will be counted as being among the God-conscious *(al-muttaqīn)*; and anyone who does this once a year will be counted as being among the doers of good *(al-muḥsinīn)*; and anyone who does this every night preceding Friday [meaning Thursday night] will be counted as being among those who devoutly pray *(al-muṣṣalīn)*, and anyone who does this [prayer] every night, I will guarantee their entry into Paradise, and no one knows the rewards of this prayer except for Allah, the Lord of the Universe, Magnificent and Lofty is He.[74]

[74] *Falāḥ al-Sāʾil*, Sayyid Ibn Ṭāwūs, pg. 246.

Second Recommended Prayer between Maghrib and ʿIshāʾ

It has been related in *Biḥār al-Anwār* and in *Falāḥ al-Sā'il* regarding the exegesis on the verse of the Qurān which states:

﴿إِنَّ نَاشِئَةَ ٱلَّيْلِ هِىَ أَشَدُّ وَطْـًٔا وَأَقْوَمُ قِيلًا ﴿٦﴾﴾

> Verily, getting up at night (for prayer) is the most effective means of subduing (oneself), and the most upright way to acquire firm control over one's actions and speech.[75]

The "getting up at night" is a special two *rakʿat* recommended prayer which one should perform between *Maghrib* and *'Ishā'*. In the first *rakʿat* after the recitation of Sūrah al-Fātiḥa, one should recite the following:

﴿الٓمٓ ﴿١﴾ ذَٰلِكَ ٱلْكِتَـٰبُ لَا رَيْبَ ۛ فِيهِ ۛ هُدًى لِّلْمُتَّقِينَ ﴿٢﴾ ٱلَّذِينَ يُؤْمِنُونَ بِٱلْغَيْبِ وَيُقِيمُونَ ٱلصَّلَوٰةَ وَمِمَّا رَزَقْنَـٰهُمْ يُنفِقُونَ ﴿٣﴾ وَٱلَّذِينَ يُؤْمِنُونَ بِمَآ أُنزِلَ إِلَيْكَ وَمَآ أُنزِلَ مِن قَبْلِكَ وَبِٱلْـَٔاخِرَةِ هُمْ يُوقِنُونَ ﴿٤﴾ أُو۟لَـٰٓئِكَ عَلَىٰ هُدًى مِّن رَّبِّهِمْ ۖ وَأُو۟لَـٰٓئِكَ هُمُ ٱلْمُفْلِحُونَ ﴿٥﴾ إِنَّ ٱلَّذِينَ كَفَرُوا۟ سَوَآءٌ عَلَيْهِمْ ءَأَنذَرْتَهُمْ أَمْ لَمْ تُنذِرْهُمْ لَا يُؤْمِنُونَ ﴿٦﴾ خَتَمَ ٱللَّهُ عَلَىٰ قُلُوبِهِمْ وَعَلَىٰ سَمْعِهِمْ ۖ وَعَلَىٰٓ أَبْصَـٰرِهِمْ غِشَـٰوَةٌ ۖ وَلَهُمْ عَذَابٌ عَظِيمٌ ﴿٧﴾ وَمِنَ ٱلنَّاسِ مَن يَقُولُ ءَامَنَّا بِٱللَّهِ وَبِٱلْيَوْمِ ٱلْـَٔاخِرِ وَمَا هُم بِمُؤْمِنِينَ ﴿٨﴾ يُخَـٰدِعُونَ ٱللَّهَ وَٱلَّذِينَ ءَامَنُوا۟ وَمَا يَخْدَعُونَ إِلَّآ

[75] Qurān, Sūrah al-Muzzammil (73), verse 6.

أَنفُسَهُمْ وَمَا يَشْعُرُونَ ﴿٩﴾ فِي قُلُوبِهِم مَّرَضٌ فَزَادَهُمُ ٱللَّهُ مَرَضًا ۖ وَلَهُمْ
عَذَابٌ أَلِيمٌۢ بِمَا كَانُوا۟ يَكْذِبُونَ ﴿١٠﴾

Alif, Lam, Mim. That is the Book, there is no doubt in it, a guidance to the God-conscious, who believe in the Unseen, and maintain the prayer, and spend out of what We have provided them with; and who believe in what has been sent down to you and what was sent down before you and are certain of the Hereafter. Those who follow their Lord's guidance, and it is they who are the felicitous. As for the faithless, it is the same to them whether you warn them or do not warn them, they will not have faith. God has set a seal on their hearts and on their hearing, and there is a blindfold on their sight, and there is a great punishment for them. And among the people are those who say, 'We have faith in God and the Last Day,' but they have no faith. They seek to deceive God and those who have faith, yet they deceive only themselves, but they are not aware. There is a sickness in their hearts; then God increased their sickness, and there is a painful punishment for them because of the lies that they used to tell.[76]

Following this, one should recite the verses known as *al-Sakhrah*[77] which are as follows:

﴿إِنَّ رَبَّكُمُ ٱللَّهُ ٱلَّذِى خَلَقَ ٱلسَّمَٰوَٰتِ وَٱلْأَرْضَ فِى سِتَّةِ أَيَّامٍ ثُمَّ
ٱسْتَوَىٰ عَلَى ٱلْعَرْشِ ۖ يُغْشِى ٱلَّيْلَ ٱلنَّهَارَ يَطْلُبُهُۥ حَثِيثًا وَٱلشَّمْسَ
وَٱلْقَمَرَ وَٱلنُّجُومَ مُسَخَّرَٰتٍۭ بِأَمْرِهِۦٓ ۗ أَلَا لَهُ ٱلْخَلْقُ وَٱلْأَمْرُ ۗ تَبَارَكَ ٱللَّهُ

[76] Qurān, Sūrah al-Baqarah (2), verses 1 - 10.

[77] Ibid., Sūrah al-A'rāf (7), verses 54 - 56.

رَبُّ ٱلۡعَٰلَمِينَ ﴿٥٤﴾ ٱدۡعُواْ رَبَّكُمۡ تَضَرُّعٗا وَخُفۡيَةًۚ إِنَّهُۥ لَا يُحِبُّ
ٱلۡمُعۡتَدِينَ ﴿٥٥﴾ وَلَا تُفۡسِدُواْ فِي ٱلۡأَرۡضِ بَعۡدَ إِصۡلَٰحِهَا وَٱدۡعُوهُ خَوۡفٗا
وَطَمَعًاۚ إِنَّ رَحۡمَتَ ٱللَّهِ قَرِيبٞ مِّنَ ٱلۡمُحۡسِنِينَ ﴿٥٦﴾﴾

Indeed, your Lord is God, who created the heavens and the earth in six days, and then assumed full authority. He draws the night's cover over the day, which pursues it swiftly, and [He created] the sun, and the moon, and the stars, [all of them] disposed by His command. Look! All creation and command belong to Him. Blessed is God, the Lord of all the worlds. Supplicate to your Lord, beseechingly and secretly. Indeed, He does not like the transgressors. And do not cause corruption on the earth after its restoration and supplicate to Him with fear and hope: indeed, God's mercy is close to the virtuous.

Then one should recite Sūrah al-Ikhlāṣ fifteen times.

In the second *rak'at*, one would recite Sūrah al-Fātiḥa followed by Āyat al-Kursī and the two verses which follow it:

﴿ٱللَّهُ لَآ إِلَٰهَ إِلَّا هُوَ ٱلۡحَيُّ ٱلۡقَيُّومُۚ لَا تَأۡخُذُهُۥ سِنَةٞ وَلَا نَوۡمٞۚ لَّهُۥ مَا فِي
ٱلسَّمَٰوَٰتِ وَمَا فِي ٱلۡأَرۡضِۗ مَن ذَا ٱلَّذِي يَشۡفَعُ عِندَهُۥٓ إِلَّا بِإِذۡنِهِۦۚ يَعۡلَمُ
مَا بَيۡنَ أَيۡدِيهِمۡ وَمَا خَلۡفَهُمۡۖ وَلَا يُحِيطُونَ بِشَيۡءٖ مِّنۡ عِلۡمِهِۦٓ إِلَّا بِمَا
شَآءَۚ وَسِعَ كُرۡسِيُّهُ ٱلسَّمَٰوَٰتِ وَٱلۡأَرۡضَۖ وَلَا يَـُٔودُهُۥ حِفۡظُهُمَاۚ وَهُوَ ٱلۡعَلِيُّ
ٱلۡعَظِيمُ ﴿٢٥٥﴾ لَآ إِكۡرَاهَ فِي ٱلدِّينِۖ قَد تَّبَيَّنَ ٱلرُّشۡدُ مِنَ ٱلۡغَيِّۚ فَمَن يَكۡفُرۡ
بِٱلطَّٰغُوتِ وَيُؤۡمِنۢ بِٱللَّهِ فَقَدِ ٱسۡتَمۡسَكَ بِٱلۡعُرۡوَةِ ٱلۡوُثۡقَىٰ لَا ٱنفِصَامَ
لَهَاۗ وَٱللَّهُ سَمِيعٌ عَلِيمٌ ﴿٢٥٦﴾ ٱللَّهُ وَلِيُّ ٱلَّذِينَ ءَامَنُواْ يُخۡرِجُهُم مِّنَ
ٱلظُّلُمَٰتِ إِلَى ٱلنُّورِۖ وَٱلَّذِينَ كَفَرُوٓاْ أَوۡلِيَآؤُهُمُ ٱلطَّٰغُوتُ يُخۡرِجُونَهُم

مِّنَ ٱلنُّورِ إِلَى ٱلظُّلُمَٰتِۗ أُوْلَٰٓئِكَ أَصْحَٰبُ ٱلنَّارِۖ هُمْ فِيهَا
خَٰلِدُونَ ﴿٢٥٧﴾

Allah - there is no god except Him - He is the Living One, the All-Sustainer. Neither drowsiness befalls Him, nor sleep. To Him belongs whatever is in the heavens and whatever is on the earth. Who is it that may intercede with Him except by His permission? He knows that which is before them and that which is behind them, and they do not comprehend anything of His knowledge except what He wishes. His seat embraces the heavens and the earth, and He is not wearied by their preservation, and He is the All-Exalted, the All-Supreme. There is no compulsion in religion: rectitude has become distinct from error. So, one who disavows the rebels and has faith in Allah has held fast to the firmest handle for which there is no breaking; and Allah is All-Hearing, All-Knowing. Allah is the Master of the faithful: He brings them out of the darknesses into the light. As for the faithless, their patrons are the rebels, who drive them out of the light into the darknesses. They shall be the inmates of the Fire, and in it they shall remain forever.[78]

After this, one should recite the end portion of Sūrah al-Baqarah[79]:

﴿لِّلَّهِ مَا فِي ٱلسَّمَٰوَٰتِ وَمَا فِي ٱلْأَرْضِۗ وَإِن تُبْدُواْ مَا فِيٓ أَنفُسِكُمْ أَوْ
تُخْفُوهُ يُحَاسِبْكُم بِهِ ٱللَّهُۖ فَيَغْفِرُ لِمَن يَشَآءُ وَيُعَذِّبُ مَن يَشَآءُۗ وَٱللَّهُ
عَلَىٰ كُلِّ شَيْءٖ قَدِيرٌ ﴿٢٨٤﴾ ءَامَنَ ٱلرَّسُولُ بِمَآ أُنزِلَ إِلَيْهِ مِن رَّبِّهِۦ
وَٱلْمُؤْمِنُونَۚ كُلٌّ ءَامَنَ بِٱللَّهِ وَمَلَٰٓئِكَتِهِۦ وَكُتُبِهِۦ وَرُسُلِهِۦ لَا نُفَرِّقُ بَيْنَ

[78] Qurān, Sūrah al-Baqarah (2), verses 255 - 257.

[79] Ibid., verses 284 - 286.

أَحَدٍ مِّن رُّسُلِهِۦ ۚ وَقَالُوا۟ سَمِعْنَا وَأَطَعْنَا ۖ غُفْرَانَكَ رَبَّنَا وَإِلَيْكَ ٱلْمَصِيرُ
﴿٢٨٥﴾ لَا يُكَلِّفُ ٱللَّهُ نَفْسًا إِلَّا وُسْعَهَا ۚ لَهَا مَا كَسَبَتْ وَعَلَيْهَا مَا
ٱكْتَسَبَتْ ۗ رَبَّنَا لَا تُؤَاخِذْنَآ إِن نَّسِينَآ أَوْ أَخْطَأْنَا ۚ رَبَّنَا وَلَا تَحْمِلْ
عَلَيْنَآ إِصْرًا كَمَا حَمَلْتَهُۥ عَلَى ٱلَّذِينَ مِن قَبْلِنَا ۚ رَبَّنَا وَلَا تُحَمِّلْنَا مَا لَا
طَاقَةَ لَنَا بِهِۦ ۖ وَٱعْفُ عَنَّا وَٱغْفِرْ لَنَا وَٱرْحَمْنَآ ۚ أَنتَ مَوْلَىٰنَا فَٱنصُرْنَا
عَلَى ٱلْقَوْمِ ٱلْكَـٰفِرِينَ ﴿٢٨٦﴾

To Allah belongs whatever is in the heavens and whatever is in the earth; and whether you disclose what is in your hearts or hide it, Allah will bring you to account for it. Then He will forgive whomever He wishes and punish whomever He wishes, and Allah has power over all things. The Apostle has faith in what has been sent down to him from his Lord, (and so do) all the faithful. Each [of them] has faith in Allah, His angels, His scriptures, and His apostles. [They declare,] 'We make no distinction between any of His apostles.' And they say, 'We hear, and we obey. Our Lord, forgive us, and towards You is the return.' Allah does not task to any soul beyond its capacity. Whatever [good] it earns is to its benefit, and whatever [evil] it incurs is to its harm. 'Our Lord! Take us not to task if we forget or make mistakes! Our Lord! Place not upon us a burden as You placed on those who were before us! Our Lord! Lay not upon us what we have no strength to bear! Excuse us and forgive us and be merciful to us! You are our Master, so help us against the faithless people!'

Then one should recite Sūrah al-Ikhlāṣ fifteen times. Once the recitations are complete, perform the *qunūt* and in it recite any supplications that you want.

The tradition ends off by stating that whoever performs this prayer and continuously recites this two *rakʿat* prayer, it will be written in the book of deeds as if one has performed 600,000 pilgrimages *(Ḥajj)*.

Points about the Recommended Prayers

1. The *Maghrib nāfilah* should be offered after *Maghrib* prayers, and one should try to offer it immediately after the *Maghrib* prayers. However, if one delays offering the *Maghrib nāfilah* until the redness in the western sky disappears, then it is better to offer the *ʿIshāʾ* prayers in that circumstance first, and then conclude with the *Maghrib nāfilah*.
2. A recommended *ṣalāt* can be offered while one is walking, or riding (on an animal or in a motor vehicle - such as a car, bus, plane, train, etc..), and if a person offers recommended prayers in these two conditions, then it is not necessary for one to be facing the *qiblah*.
3. Even if a person has obligatory *(wājib) ṣalāt* pending which have not been performed yet, one is still permitted to recite the recommended prayers - however, a believer should not delay in performing one's obligations.

Differences Between Obligatory and Recommended Prayers

1. All the recommended prayers are performed as two rakʿat prayers except for *Ṣalāt al-Witr* in the night prayers which is only one *rakʿat*, and *Ṣalāt al-Aʿrābī* which is comprised of an

individual two *rakʿat ṣalāt* followed by two sets of four *rakʿat* prayers.[80]

---

[80] *Al-ʿUrwah al-Wuthqā*, vol. 2, pg. 111, ruling 6. In a tradition found in *al-Miṣbāḥ* narrated from Zayd ibn Thābit he says: "A man from the desert-dwelling community *(aʿrāb)* came to the Messenger of Allāh ﷺ and said to him: 'May my father and my mother be ransomed for your sake, O Messenger of Allāh! We live in a desert far away from Medina and we are not able to come to you every Friday (for the Friday prayers); therefore can you guide us to an action which will entail the reward of *Ṣalāt al-Jumuʿah,* and so when I go back to my family, I can relate it to them?' The Messenger of Allāh ﷺ said to him: 'When the midday time starts, perform a two *rakʿat* prayer - in the first *rakʿat*, recite Sūrah al-Ḥamd once, followed by Sūrah al-Falaq seven times; and in the second *rakʿat*, recite Sūrah al-Ḥamd once, followed by Sūrah al-Nās seven times; when you have completed this and performed the *salām* [to end the prayer], then recite Ayat al-Kursī seven times. Following this, stand and offer eight [more] *rakʿat* of prayers with two *salām* [meaning two prayers of four *rakʿat* each] - in the first *rakʿat* of each prayer, recite Sūrah al-Ḥamd once, followed by Sūrah al-Naṣr once and then Sūrah al-Ikhlāṣ twenty-five times, and once you have completed your prayers, then say the following seven times:

سُبْحَانَ اللّٰهِ رَبِّ الْعَرْشِ الْكَرِيمِ وَ لاَ حَوْلَ وَ لاَ قُوَّةَ إِلاَّ بِاللّٰهِ الْعَلِيِّ الْعَظِيمِ

I take an oath by the One who chose me for Prophethood that there is not a single believing man, nor believing woman who performs this *ṣalāt* on Friday just as I have instructed it to be performed, except that I guarantee them Paradise; and that person does not stand where they stand [to perform this prayer] except that they are forgiven their sins and [also] their parents are forgiven their sins.'"

2. Regarding the recommended prayers, except for some of them, it is not obligatory to recite a second chapter of the Qurān (in the position of *qiyām* - meaning that one only needs to recite Sūrah al-Fātiḥa).[81]

3. It is permissible to intentionally break a recommended prayer, even for no reason.[82]

4. Unintentionally performing an additional *rukn* (such as a *rukūʿ* or *sajdah*) does not invalidate the recommended prayer.[83]

5. While performing the recommended prayers, if a person begins to doubt whether they have performed one or two *rakʿat*, then their prayers will not be invalidated and they are free to choose either doubt [either having performed one or two *rakʿat*] and continue in one's prayers [meaning that one can count it as being the first or second *rakʿat*].[84]

6. It is permissible to pray the recommended prayers sitting down, however it is better that one counts two *rakʿat* of recommended prayers performed sitting down as one *rakʿat*.[85]

7. A person should not perform the recommended prayers for *Dhuhr* and *ʿAṣr* while on a journey, however recommended prayers for *ʿIshāʾ* can be performed with the intention that 'perhaps it is something good to perform.'[86] (The *nāfilah* for *Fajr* and *Maghrib* prayers can be performed as these *ṣalāt* are not shortened.)

---

81 *Al-ʿUrwah al-Wuthqā*, vol. 2, pg. 111, ruling 7.

82 Ibid.

83 Ibid.

84 Ibid., ruling 1167.

85 Ibid., ruling 766.

86 Ibid., ruling 767.

8. Regarding the obligatory prayers, it is better that a person performs them in the masjid, however when it comes to the recommended prayers, this same recommendation is not there.

9. If one unintentionally performs extra or less actions (which are required in the *ṣalāt*) during the recommended prayers, then one is not obliged to perform the *sajdah* of *sahw.*

10. If a person was not able to perform the recommended prayers when their time set in, then one can still perform them after their time has lapsed.

11. Recommended prayers can be performed in any state - walking, riding (in a vehicle), etc.; and if a person performs them in this state, then one is not obligated (only for the recommended prayers) to face the *qiblah.*[87]

12. The recommended prayers can be performed standing, sitting, while walking, etc.; and when doing so, the method of performing *rukūʿ* and *sajdah* can be simply indicating the action by a movement of the head, however as far as possible, one should make the best effort to face the *qiblah.*

13. In the recommended prayers, complete stillness and motionlessness of the body is not a condition.

14. A person can make a promise to Allah ﷻ *(nadhr)* that they will perform a recommended prayer (if what they have asked for is fulfilled) and this prayer can be performed sitting or standing, while moving or stationary - however a person must be careful that when one makes the *nadhr*, one does not make an intention to perform the recommended prayer sitting [or in a specific position/format].

---

[87] *Al-ʿUrwah al-Wuthqā*, vol. 2, pg. 111, ruling 781.

Appendix I: Prophet Yūnus 🕊 and Divine Examinations

The sixth and final story of the Prophets and previous generations which occurs in this chapter (Sūrah al-Ṣāffāt) concerns Prophet Yūnus 🕊 and his repentant community. It is interesting to note that in regards to the five previously mentioned communities, namely those of Prophet Nūḥ 🕊, Prophet Ibrāhīm 🕊, Prophet Mūsā 🕊 and Prophet Hārūn 🕊, Prophet Ilyās 🕊, and Prophet Lūṭ 🕊, in the end none of their respective communities awoke from their spiritual slumber, and thus the Divine retribution of Allah ﷻ came over them and Allah ﷻ ended up saving these great Prophets (and their few followers and believers) from experiencing the punishment.

However, in this narrative, the outcome is quite the opposite as by witnessing the impending signs of Divine punishment, the disbelieving nation of Prophet Yūnus 🕊, awoke from their spiritual negligence and turned back in repentance. Therefore Allah ﷻ covered them with His grace and allowed them to partake in material and spiritual bounties. In addition, even Prophet Yūnus 🕊 himself, who due to the action he performed which is regarded as a *tark al-awlā* as he prematurely left his community, fell into difficulties and grief. For this, the word *ibq* was used to refer to him - which is a word normally employed for a servant which flees from his master!

This story is a lesson addressed to everyone to learn from - not only the polytheistic Arabs at the time of the Prophet of Islām 🕊 - but all of humanity from the entire course of history - that do we want to end up like the five communities which were previously spoken about in this chapter or do we want to be like the community of Prophet Yūnus 🕊? Are we seeking to attract the painful punishments of the previous generations, or do we want to go after a good and blissful outcome? The choice is up to us!

In any case, within various chapters of the Noble Qurān, including Sūrah al-Anbiyāʾ, Sūrah Yūnus, Sūrah al-Qalam, and this chapter (Sūrah al-Ṣāffāt), the story of this great Prophet - meaning Prophet Yūnus 🕊 has been mentioned and in every portion [of his story as narrated in the Noble Qurān], a unique portion of him and his condition is displayed. However, as for the account given in Sūrah al-Ṣāffāt, it primarily focuses on Prophet Yūnus 🕊 fleeing his community, the challenges he faced and his eventual rescue.

First off, just as with the previous stories, the narration begins by speaking about his station of Messengership *(Risālah)* and we read:

$$\text{﴿وَإِنَّ يُونُسَ لَمِنَ الْمُرْسَلِينَ ﴿١٣٩﴾﴾}$$

And Yūnus was most surely from among the Messengers.[88]

Just like the other Prophets, Prophet Yūnus 🕊 began his invitation by calling the people to the oneness of Allah 🕊 and to leave idol worshipping; and from that point, his call went on to fight against the various corruptions which were taking place in his society.

However, his intolerant community whose spiritual eyes and ears were sealed and who were busy blindly following their elders refused to submit to his message.

In the way of a loving, caring and concerned father for his children, Prophet Yūnus 🕊 continued to warn his community, however in the face of his logical discussions, he heard nothing other than sophistry from the detractors, and it was only a small number of people, which presumably was not more than two - one devout worshipper and one scholar - who ended up believing in him.

Prophet Yūnus 🕊 carried out many efforts in propagation that he almost gave up hope in his people, and it is mentioned in some of the *aḥādīth* that on the advice of the devout worshipper who

---

[88] Qurān, Sūrah al-Ṣāffāt (37), verse 139.

accepted his message and through his own analysis of the situation of his misled community, he decided to imprecate his community.[89]

This plan of his finally began to materialize and Prophet Yūnus عليه السلام imprecated against his people, and it was at this stage of the narrative that it was revealed to him that 'at such and such a time, the Divine punishment will come down upon the people.'

When the promised time of the punishment began to approach, Prophet Yūnus عليه السلام, along with the devout worshipper proceeded to leave the people of the community, while he was in a state of rage. They continued walking until they reached towards the seashore and saw a huge ship which was carrying both many people and cargo, so they asked if they would be permitted to embark on the boat - and they were given permission.

This is what the Qurān refers to in the next verse and states:

﴿إِذْ أَبَقَ إِلَى الْفُلْكِ الْمَشْحُونِ ١٤٠﴾

When he ran away to a ship completely laden.[90]

The meaning of the word *abaqa* which comes from the root *abāq* means 'a slave who has run away from his master' and thus, it being used here is a point of astonishment and it shows us that the act of a very small *tark al-awlā* by one of the lofty-ranking Prophets is taken extremely seriously and its reproach by Allah ﷻ is carried out - such that His own Prophet is referred to as a slave who has run away from his master!

Without a doubt, Prophet Yūnus عليه السلام was infallible *(ma'ṣūm)* and never did he commit any sin, however it was better for him to still endure things and stay with his community until the last moments just before the punishment of the Divine comes down, as perhaps his community may have come out of their state of negligence.

---

[89] *Tafsīr al-Burhān*, vol. 4, pg. 35.

[90] Qurān, Sūrah al-Ṣāffāt (37), verse 140.

It is true that according to some of the narrations, he worked on propagating the message for forty years, however still it would have been better for him to stay a few more days or months among his people until Allah's command came to him, and because he did not do so, he is compared to a run-away slave.

In any case, Prophet Yūnus ﷺ got on a boat, and according to some narrations, an extremely large fish propped itself up directly in front of the boat with his mouth wide open - as if he was looking for food. Those who were on the boat said: 'It looks like there is a sinner in our midst! He needs to be the food for this fish. To determine who will go, we will draw lots.' When they ended up drawing lots, the results came that Prophet Yūnus ﷺ was the one who had to go!

According to the traditions, the people on the ship drew lots a total of three times and each time, the name of Prophet Yūnus ﷺ came up and therefore Prophet Yūnus ﷺ had no other choice but to throw himself into the mouth of this massive fish.

In the verses under review, the Qurān through employing one short sentence, refers to this entire event and states:

﴿فَسَاهَمَ فَكَانَ مِنَ ٱلْمُدْحَضِينَ ١٤١﴾

> So, he shared (with them), but was of those who were cast off.[91]

The word *sāhama* comes from the root *sahm* and its original meaning is an arrow, while the word *musāhamah* means drawing lots (lottery) as at the time of drawing lots, they would write the names of each person on thin strips of wood [which resemble arrows], mix them up all together and then one of these thin strips of wood would be chosen and whoever's name was written on the stick would be the one who was chosen to perform a certain task.

---

[91] Qurān, Sūrah al-Ṣāffāt (37), verse 141.

The word *mudhiḍh* comes from the word *idhāḍh* and it means to nullify something, eroding something away and conquering something, and in this verse its meaning is: the draw chose his name.

Another explanation has also been given which states that the sea became very unstable and the cargo in the ship seemed to be too much to bear and at every instant, there was a fear of everyone drowning and thus, they had no choice but to lighten the load that they were carrying, and this meant to throw some people off the boat into the sea. The one who was chosen, by way of drawing lots, was none other than Prophet Yūnus 🕊 and so they ended up throwing him into the sea and it was then that the giant fish came and swallowed him whole.

At this point the Qurān states:

$$﴿فَٱلْتَقَمَهُ ٱلْحُوتُ وَهُوَ مُلِيمٌ ۝﴾$$

So, the fish swallowed him while he did that for which he blamed himself.[92]

The word *iltaqamahu* comes from the word *iltiqām* and it means 'to swallow'; the word *mulīm* comes from the word *lūm* and it means 'to reproach or rebuke', and it conveys the meaning behind the word *lā'im* and in this passage it means 'he reprimanded himself'.

It is an established fact that this reprimanding and rebuking was **not** due to the performance of a major or minor sin - rather, it was due to the *tark al-awlā* that he had performed which was him having left his community prematurely.

However, the same Allah who can maintain fire burning under water and can protect a glass which is beside a rock, ordered this large aquatic mammal through His command over nature to ensure that not the least amount of harm reaches His servant, Prophet

---

[92] Qurān, Sūrah al-Ṣāffāt (37), verse 142.

Yūnus ﷺ; and that he must endure a period of unparalleled form of imprisonment so that he may realize his *tark al-awlā* and make amends for it.

It has been mentioned in a *ḥadīth* that:

أَوْحىَ اللّٰهُ تَعالىٰ اِلىٰ الْحُوتِ لاتَكْسِرْ مِنْهُ عَظْماً وَ لاتَقْطَعْ لَهُ وَصْلاً

> Allah, the Most High, revealed [communicated] to the fish that it must not break a single bone in his (Yūnus's ﷺ) body, and that it must not sever a single connection of his body.[93]

Prophet Yūnus ﷺ very quickly realized what was happening to him, and with his entire presence he turned back towards Allah ﷻ [in repentance] from his *tark al-awlā* and sought forgiveness and asked for clemency from His sacred presence.

It is at this point in the narrative that the famous and meaningful recitation (*dhikr)* came out from the mouth of Prophet Yūnus ﷺ which is narrated in verse 87 of Sūrah al-Anbiyā', which among the people of spirituality, is known as the *Dhikr Yūnusiyyah* which states:

﴿لاَ إِلٰهَ إِلاَّ أَنْتَ سُبْحَانَكَ إِنِّي كُنْتُ مِنَ الظَّالِمِينَ ۝٨٧﴾

> There is no god but You, glory be to You; surely I am of those who make themselves to suffer loss.[94]

This sincere confession and his verbal declaration of glorification which was infused with true remorse fulfilled its goal and just as it is mentioned in verse 88 of Sūrah al-Anbiyā' that:

---

93 *Tafsīr al-Kabīr*, vol. 26, pg. 165. A similar understanding, with slight variances, can be gleamed from *Tafsīr al-Burhān*, vol. 4, pg. 37.

94 Qurān, Sūrah al-Anbiyā' (21), verse 87.

﴿فَاسْتَجَبْنَا لَهُ وَ نَجَّيْنَاهُ مِنَ الْغَمِّ وَ كَذَٰلِكَ نُنْجِي الْمُؤْمِنِينَ ﴿٨٨﴾﴾

So, We responded to him and delivered him from the grief and thus do We deliver the believers.[95]

At this point, let us return to the verse under review and see what it says. In one short sentence, we read that had Prophet Yūnus ﷺ not been of those who glorified Allah ﷻ...

﴿فَلَوْ لَا أَنَّهُ كَانَ مِنَ الْمُسَبِّحِينَ ﴿١٤٣﴾﴾

But had it not been that he was of those who glorify (Us).[96]

Allah ﷻ continues by saying:

﴿لَلَبِثَ فِي بَطْنِهِ إِلَىٰ يَوْمِ يُبْعَثُونَ ﴿١٤٤﴾﴾

He would certainly have tarried in its belly to the day when they are raised.[97]

Here, Allah ﷻ is telling us that this temporary prison term of Prophet Yūnus ﷺ would have been transformed into a life-sentence and that this prison which would have been his permanent place of incarceration would have eventually been his final resting place!

At this point some may ask, if Prophet Yūnus ﷺ was to remain in the belly of the fish until the Day of Resurrection (supposing that he did not glorify Allah ﷻ and ask forgiveness from Him), would he have remained alive [through the power of Allah ﷻ] or would he have eventually died? Various commentators of the Qurān have given the below possibilities to this question:

---

[95] Qurān, Sūrah al-Anbiyā᾽ (21), verse 88.

[96] Ibid., Sūrah al-Ṣāffāt (37), verse 143.

[97] Ibid., verse 144.

1. Both (meaning Prophet Yūnus 🕮 and the fish) would have remained alive and Prophet Yūnus 🕮 would have remained in the belly of the fish, imprisoned, until the Day of Judgement.
2. Prophet Yūnus 🕮 would have died and his body would have remained in the belly of the fish as a free-moving graveyard, and the fish would have remained alive.
3. Both Prophet Yūnus 🕮 and the fish would have died and the stomach of the fish would have ended up being the grave of Prophet Yūnus 🕮 while the earth would have been the grave of the fish - Prophet Yūnus 🕮 in the stomach of the fish and the fish in the stomach of the earth, and they would have remained like this until the Day of Judgement.

We cannot use the verse under discussion to corroborate any of these opinions, however various other verses do tell us that at the end of this world, everything which was created will cease to exist and this shows us that it is not possible for Prophet Yūnus 🕮 or the fish to have remained alive until the Day of Judgement. Therefore, from the three commentaries given as possible answers, the third opinion is closer to what the reality is.[98]

Yet another possibility exists which is that this phrase used may have only been an allusion to a long period of time - meaning that he would have remained in this prison in the belly of the fish for a very long time, just as such phrases are sometimes used in our common daily usage when one says: "You're going to have to wait until the end of the world if you want to know that!"

However, we should not forget that all of this would have taken place had he not gone forth to glorify and turn back to Allah 🕮,

---

[98] It is worthy to note that the late commentator of the Qurān, al-Ṭabarsī, who normally quotes varying opinions under his commentary of verses has only referred to one opinion in this regard and he says: "The stomach of the fish would have been his grave until the Day of Resurrection."

however this did not happen and therefore, under the shadow of his glorification of Allah ﷻ, he was enveloped in His special forgiveness.

The Qurān then states:

﴿فَنَبَذْنَاهُ بِالْعَرَاءِ وَهُوَ سَقِيمٌ ﴿١٤٥﴾﴾

Then We cast him on to the vacant surface of the earth while he was sick.[99]

This massive sea creature made its way towards the barren shoreline, and by the command of Allah ﷻ, released whatever was inside of him, and it was seen that this amazing prison maintained the body of Prophet Yūnus عليه السلام and brought him back out alive - albeit ill and weak.

We do not know how long Prophet Yūnus عليه السلام spent in the belly of that fish, but what is clear is that however long it was, it was something which clearly affected him in many ways. It is correct that the order of Allah ﷻ was given that Prophet Yūnus عليه السلام should not be devoured by a fish; however this does not mean that he should not face any of the effects of being in such a prison. Therefore, a group of commentators of the Qurān have written that he made his way out of the belly of the fish just like a baby chick, weak and featherless, makes its way out of an egg - he literally did not have the ability to even move!

Even at this point, the grace of the Divine went to Prophet Yūnus عليه السلام as his sick and weakened body lie on the shores and the beating rays of the sun bore down on his body troubling him. He needed a thin covering over him so that his body could rest and recover under the heat of the sun, and it is this point that the Qurān states:

﴿وَأَنْبَتْنَا عَلَيْهِ شَجَرَةً مِنْ يَقْطِينٍ ﴿١٤٦﴾﴾

---

[99] Qurān, Sūrah al-Ṣāffāt (37), verse 145.

And We caused to grow up for him a gourd plant.[100]

The word *yaqṭīn*, just as many of the scholars of the ʿArabic language and commentators of the Qurān have stated refers to any type of plant which has no stem or stalk and has open leaves, such as a melon plant, squash, zucchini, cucumber, and other such plants. However, most of the commentators of the Qurān and the narrators of *ḥadīth* have reiterated that the specific meaning of this word used in the verse is that of pumpkin. It must be noted that in the language of the Arabs, the word *shajarah* can be used both for vegetation which has stems or stalks and those without stems. In other words, it is a general word used for any type of tree or vegetation.

We see a *ḥadīth* from the Noble Prophet of Islām ﷺ in which it has been narrated that a person came to him and said:

اِنَّكَ تُحِبُّ الْقَرْعَ؟

Do you like [to eat] squash?

The Prophet ﷺ replied to this person:

أَجَلْ! هِيَ شَجَرَةُ اَخِي يُونُسَ

Of course! That is the plant of my brother Yūnus![101]

It has been stated that not only does the pumpkin have large, open leaves which are full of water, but also that one can easily construct a canopy from them and that flies tend to not rest on them. Since the skin on Prophet Yūnus' ﷺ body had become thinned due to the time spent in the belly of the fish, when he would sit or lie down, he would feel pain throughout his entire body and therefore he covered himself in a bed of these large leaves from the pumpkin

---

[100] Qurān, Sūrah al-Ṣaffāt (37), verse 146.

[101] *Tafsīr Rūḥ al-Bayān*, vol. 7, pg. 489.

plant so that his body would be protected from the heat of the sun and he would not feel the pain due to his frailty.

Perhaps Allah ﷻ wanted the lesson which Prophet Yūnus ﷺ learnt while he was in the belly of the fish to reach its climax at this stage, by now having to bare the scorching heat of the sun on the thinned skin of his body, so that in the future when it comes to the station of guidance and leadership in seeking to save his own community from the burning fire of hell, he would work even harder and put in even greater efforts; and indeed, this is the same understanding which we are given from the narrations.[102]

At this point of the discussion, we leave aside Prophet Yūnus ﷺ and focus on his community and what was happening to them.

At the time when Prophet Yūnus ﷺ left his community filled with anger and rage, and the introductory stages of the punishment of the Divine began to manifest, they began to feel the intensity of the tribulations and came to their senses. They ran towards the scholar who was in their midst and sought the means of repentance through his guidance and leadership.

In some of the *aḥādīth* it has been mentioned that they all went out together as a group into the open desert and got into groups - the women and children and the animals and their offspring, and then began weeping over their bad actions. The sound of their cries increased in intensity, and they sincerely asked repentance for their sins and shortcomings regarding how they treated the Prophet of God, Prophet Yūnus ﷺ.

It was at this point that the curtains of punishment were pushed aside, and some tumultuous event overtook the mountains in that region and this congregation of believers who had sincerely asked for repentance were saved by the grace of Allah.[103]

---

[102] *Tafsīr Nūr al-Thaqalayn*, vol. 4, pg. 436, trad. 116.

[103] This *ḥadīth* has been narrated in *Tafsīr al-Burhān*, vol. 4, pg. 35, as coming from Imām al-Ṣādiq ﷺ.

It was after this event that Prophet Yūnus 🕮 returned to his community to see what form of punishment had befallen his people.

When he arrived, he was thrown into a state of bewilderment that how is it that on the day when he left, they were all engulfed in their idol worshipping, however today they are all submitters to the Oneness of God and are worshipping God alone!?

At this point in the story, the Qurān states:

$$﴿وَ أَرْسَلْناهُ إِلى مِائَةِ أَلْفٍ أَوْ يَزِيدُونَ ﴿١٤٧﴾﴾$$

And We sent him to a [community of a] hundred thousand, rather they exceeded [that number].[104]

Allah 🕮 continues and He then states:

$$﴿فَآمَنُوا فَمَتَّعْناهُمْ إِلى حِينٍ ﴿١٤٨﴾﴾$$

And they believed, so We gave them provision until a time.[105]

Their outer acceptance of the true faith and turning back in repentance had been carried out previously, however the acceptance of the true faith in Allah 🕮 and His Prophet Yūnus 🕮 and his teachings and ordinances only took a manifest reality after Prophet Yūnus 🕮 returned to them.

It should be noted that from the verses of the Qurān we deduce that this renewed responsibility which he was given was towards his **same** community, and the opinion which some scholars have that Prophet Yūnus' 🕮 responsibility of guidance was directed towards a new community of people does not fit with the apparent reading of the verses of the Qurān. From one aspect, we read in the verse that:

---

[104] Qurān, Sūrah al-Ṣāffāt (37), verse 147.
[105] Ibid., verse 148.

$$﴿فَآمَنُوا فَمَتَّعْنَاهُمْ إِلَى حِينٍ ۝﴾$$

And they believed, so We gave them provision until a time.[106]

This means that this community which Prophet Yūnus ※ was charged with guiding were individuals who had just accepted true faith and that We (Allah) allowed them to reside on the Earth for an appointed period.

From another perspective, these same phrases have been mentioned in Sūrah Yūnus in which we read the following about his community:

$$﴿فَلَوْلَا كَانَتْ قَرْيَةٌ ءَامَنَتْ فَنَفَعَهَآ إِيمَنُهَآ إِلَّا قَوْمَ يُونُسَ لَمَّآ ءَامَنُواْ$$
$$كَشَفْنَا عَنْهُمْ عَذَابَ ٱلْخِزْيِ فِي ٱلْحَيَوٰةِ ٱلدُّنْيَا وَمَتَّعْنَاهُمْ إِلَى$$
$$حِينٍ ۝﴾$$

And wherefore was there not a town which should believe so that their belief should have profited them but the people of Yūnus? When they believed, We removed from them the chastisement of disgrace in this world's life, and We gave them provision until a time.[107]

Therefore, from this it becomes clear that the meaning of the phrase ilā ḥīn - 'until a specific time' means the end of their natural life.

As for why is it that in the above-mentioned verses we read, 'one hundred thousand, or more' and what is the meaning or measure of 'more,' the various commentators of the Qurān have offered differing commentaries on this point. However, what is clear is that such phrases are employed to show emphasis and

---

[106] Qurān, Sūrah al-Ṣāffāt (37), verse 148.
[107] Ibid., Sūrah Yūnus (10), verse 98.

vastness of something - not to bring about further doubts and confusions.[108]

Points to Consider

Brief Review of the Life of Prophet Yūnus 🕮

Prophet Yūnus 🕮 was the son of Mittai and his nickname was *Dhū Nūn* (Companion of the Fish) and this title was given to him due to the historical event which was mentioned previously about him being swallowed whole by a fish.

He is one of the well-known Prophets who apparently came after Prophet Mūsā 🕮 and Prophet Hārūn 🕮, and some scholars consider him to be from the progeny of Prophet Hūd 🕮. His responsibility was to guide those who remained from the people of Thamūd [who had been destroyed previously], and he was born and brought up in ʿIrāq in the region of Naynawā (Nineveh).[109]

Some have stated that he came on the scene around 825 years before the birth of Prophet ʿIsā 🕮 and even today, close to the city of Kūfa in ʿIrāq, near the river bank, there is a grave which is commonly believed to be that of Prophet Yūnus 🕮.

---

[108] According to this opinion, the *aw* mentioned in this phrase is in the meaning of *bal* or 'rather.'

[109] Naynawā is the name shared by many geographic regions. First off, it is a city near Mosul (or what is known as Qaṣbah Mosul); it is also an area in the vicinity of Kūfa towards the direction of Kerbalāʾ; and it is also a city in Asia Minor in the country of Assyria near to the Tigris river - according to the *Dahkhuda Encyclopedia*. Other scholars have written that Naynawā is the largest among the cities of Assyria which was built on the Eastern side of the Tigris facing opposite to the city of Mosul - according to *The Qurān Encyclopedia*.

It has been mentioned in some books that he was a prophet from the Tribes of Israel and was brought forth as a Prophet after Prophet Sulaymān ﷺ for the people of Naynawā.

In the Book of Jonah in the *Old Testament* there is a detailed discussion regarding Prophet Yūnus ﷺ.[110]

According to this narration, he was entrusted with going to the large city of Naynawā and to stand up to the wicked people of this city. From here the story takes a different turn which closely resembles that which has been mentioned in the Qurān with this difference that according to the Islamic narrations, Prophet Yūnus ﷺ accepted the invitation of the people and fulfilled his responsibility in this regards and after he saw that the people were rejecting his invitation, he then imprecated against them and left them and from there, the story of the ship and the fish take form.

However, in the *Old Testament*, there are some very harsh words used against him which states:

> But Jonah ran away from the LORD and headed for Tarshish. He went down to Joppa, where he found a ship bound for that port. After paying the fare, he went aboard and sailed for Tarshish to flee from the LORD.

Even more astonishing than this is that we see the *Torah* states the following:

> When God saw what they did and how they turned from their evil ways, he relented and did not bring on them the destruction he had threatened. But to Jonah this seemed very wrong, and he became angry. He prayed to the LORD, "Isn't this what I said, LORD, when I was still at home? That is what I tried to forestall by fleeing to Tarshish. I knew that you are a gracious and compassionate God, slow to anger and abounding in love, a God who relents from sending

[110] The entire passage from the Old Testament is presented in Appendix I of this book.

> calamity. Now, LORD, take away my life, for it is better for me to die than to live." But the LORD replied, "Is it right for you to be angry?[111]

From other parts of the story mentioned in the *Torah* we see that Prophet Yūnus was once again given the responsibility of guidance. During the first instance, he refrained from fulfilling his obligations and was thus faced with his painful outcome [of being imprisoned in the belly of a fish]; while on the second round of his responsibility to go back to the same people of Naynawā, he found the people of the city had awoken from their spiritual slumber and negligence of God, and that they had finally brought about true faith in Allah, and that they had turned back to Him from their sins and were thus enveloped in the forgiveness of the Divine, and Prophet Yūnus got upset at Allah for why He forgave them so!?

If we compare that which is mentioned in the Qurān and the Islamic traditions with that which is contained in the present-day *Old Testament*, it becomes explicitly clear to what extent textual changes have occurred in the *Old Testament* as they have brought down the level and status of such a lofty Prophet of Allah. As we have seen, at times they attribute the sin of him refusing to fulfill his responsibility of propagating a message to his people; in another instance he is shown as being angry and upset at the forgiveness and mercy of Allah over his repentant nation - this should be a clear indication of the status of the *Old Testament* in our eyes and that nothing of it can be trusted or relied upon [as being the word of Allah].

In any case, he is without a doubt one of the major Prophets which the Qurān has spoken about in glowing terms.

---

[111] *Old Testament*, Book of Jonah, Section one, two, three and four.

How did Yūnus ﷺ Remain Alive in the Belly of the Fish?

As we have stated, we do not have any clear proof at hand to state exactly how long Prophet Yūnus ﷺ stayed in the belly of the fish. Was it merely a few hours, a few days or maybe a few months - it is not clear at all. However, what we see in some of the traditions are a few opinions including that he was in the belly for only about nine hours; other traditions mention three days, while other *ḥadīth* point to more than that, and there is even one opinion which states that he was in the belly of the fish for a period of forty days, however we have no definite proof for any of these varied opinions. The only thing that we have in hand which is contained in the commentary of the Qurān of ʿAlī ibn Ibrāhīm is a *ḥadīth* from the Commander of the Faithful ʿAlī ﷺ in which he states that the period of Prophet Yūnus' ﷺ stay in the belly of the fish was nine hours.[112]

It should be noted that some of the commentators of the Qurān from among the Ahl al-Sunnah have mentioned that he was in the belly of the fish for only one hour.[113]

However whatever the period was, without a doubt this stay in the belly of a fish was something quite extraordinary as we know that a human being cannot live in an environment which has no oxygen for more than a few minutes, and when we see that a fetus resides in the womb of its mother for months this is due to the fact that the baby's respiratory system has not yet been fully developed and is not functional, and therefore whatever oxygen it needs to sustain itself comes from the blood of the baby's mother.

Therefore, we can state that the exceptional event of Prophet Yūnus ﷺ is nothing short of a miracle, but of course this is not the

---

[112] *Tafsīr ʿAlī ibn Ibrāhīm*, according to the narration in *Tafsīr Nūr al-Thaqalayn*, vol. 4, pg. 436.

[113] *Tafsīr al-Qurṭubī*, vol. 8, pg. 5567.

first miracle which has been mentioned in the Qurān. That same God who protected Prophet Ibrāhīm ☀ from the depths of the fire; the same God who saved Prophet Mūsā ☀ and the Tribes of Israel by making a dry path through the sea and saved them from drowning; the same God who granted security to Prophet Nūḥ ☀ through the means of a simple ark which he made and was protected from the great deluge and allowed him to disembark on the dry land - is the same God who has the power to put one of His chosen servants in the belly of a massive fish for a protracted period of time and protect him while he was in there.

Of course, the presence of such an enormous fish is not something uncommon - even today we see the massive fish known as the whale can exceed 30 meters in length and is perhaps one of the largest creatures on the face of this Earth - and the weight of its liver alone can exceed one ton!

This same sūrah contains the stories of the previous Prophets in which they found salvation through the most miraculous of ways from the grips of tribulations, and Prophet Yūnus ☀ is merely the last of them in the chain of Prophets mentioned.

A Grand Lesson in a Small Story

We know that the rationale for such stories contained within the Noble Qurān are for [our] training and education because the Qurān is not simply a book of stories - rather, it is a book sent to spiritually build the human being and train them.

From the remarkable outcome of the story of Prophet Yūnus ☀, we can derive many major lessons.

1. Any sort of disobedience [to the orders of Allah ☀] - even if it is a *tark al-awlā* - from a major Prophet in the presence of Allah ☀ is a serious act and will result in retribution. However, as the station of Prophethood is something extremely lofty, one minor slip of spiritual negligence

regarding such individuals can be a major sin [although it is not a sin] which would emanate from a non-Prophet and it is for this reason that we have seen that in this story, Allah ﷻ has referred to him as a run-away slave. In addition, it has been mentioned in the traditions that others who were in the boat with him stated: 'There is one sinner amongst us!' Eventually, Allah ﷻ made him enter the fearful prison of the stomach of the fish and it was only after his remorse and repentance and turning back towards Allah ﷻ, that with a pain-filled and sickened body, was he freed from that prison. All of this was carried out so that everyone may come to know that such disobedience will not be tolerated from anyone and that even the lofty status of the Prophets and close friends of Allah ﷻ fall into this rule that they too must be obedient servants to His commands and that if they are not, then we are made to realize that Allah ﷻ shares no relationship or bond with anyone. This shows the high status of this great Prophet that Allah ﷻ even deals with him in such a strict fashion.

2. In this same story, in the portion which has been narrated in Sūrah al-Anbiyā', verse 87, we see that the path to salvation for a true believer is to show remorse and grief, and also to suffer difficulties such as what Yūnus ﵇ traversed in his life, and it is the confession of one's incorrect actions in the presence of the All Truth, the glorification, sanctification, repentance and turning back towards Him which will save an individual.

3. This event shows how a sinful community which was deserving of a Divine punishment can - even at the last moment - alter their own history and save themselves; and fall into the lap of mercy and compassion from the Divine - on the condition that they realize their situation before it is

too late and choose a wise scholar to lead them to the correct path.

4. True faith in Allah ﷻ and sincere repentance from one's sins, in addition to the spiritual benefits and blessings which it brings, also carries with it material worldly blessings for the human being as well. It brings about material growth and the further ability to live on the Earth, and results in a lengthened lifespan and an opportunity to benefit from the gift of life. This outcome is also something which can be seen in the story of Prophet Nūḥ ؑ which is covered in the commentary of Sūrah Nūḥ.[114]

5. The power of Allah ﷻ is so encompassing and expansive that nothing is hard for Him, to the extent that He can safeguard a human being in the mouth and belly of a massive frightful creature and bring that same person out unharmed. This clearly shows that all the means of this world are according to His Will, and everything submits to His will.

Reply To One Question

At this point a question comes up which is: In the recounting of other previous nations in the verses of the Qurān, it has been mentioned that when the punishment came down upon them (that form of punishment which is sent to completely eradicate transgressive communities), repentance and remorse were of no use; then how was it possible that the nation of Prophet Yūnus ؑ were an exception to this rule?

---

[114] This has been translated as Exegesis of the Qurān: Sūrah al-Mulk to Sūrah al-Mursalāt (A Translation of *Tafsīr Namuneh* - 29th Section of the Noble Qurān) - published by the Islamic Humanitarian Service (www.al-haqq.com) and co-published by the Islamic Publishing House (www.iph.ca).

Regarding a reply to this question, there are two answers which can be given:

1. The punishment had not yet started to be meted out to those people - all that was seen was the brief, introductory signs to an impending punishment which included various types of warnings, such that they may be able to see these and make amends and so that before the actual punishment descends upon them, they would turn in repentance and bring about true faith.

2. The second response is that this punishment was not going to be a punishment to completely eradicate them - rather, it was more of a wake-up call sort of introductory punishment which was to come before the actual final retribution which had been given to previous nations as well, such that before they lose the opportunity, they awaken from their spiritual slumber and choose the path of piety. These sorts of punishments had been seen in previous generations as well - such as what happened to the people of Pharaoh before he and his army were drowned.

Drawing Lots and Its Permissibility in Islām

There are some traditions regarding drawing lots and whether they are permissible in Islām. Imām al-Ṣādiq ﷺ has stated:

أَيُّ قَضِيَّةٍ أَعْدَلُ مِنَ الْقُرْعَةِ إِذَا فُوِّضَ الْأَمْرُ إِلَى اللهِ عَزَّوَجَلَّ يَقُولُ:
﴿فَسَاهَمَ فَكَانَ مِنَ ٱلْمُدْحَضِينَ ١٤١﴾

Which form of coming to a solution [on a matter of confusion] is more just than drawing lots? When one places their complete reliance upon Allah, the noble and grand, just

> as Allah has said: ﴾So he shared (with them) but was among those who are cast off.﴿[115]

This points to the fact that drawing lots [to decide something], when an issue comes up which is difficult to determine what one should do and for which there is no other way to conclude, can be done but one must first place all of their trust on Allah ﷻ - who is truthfully the road to resolution, just as has been seen in the story of Prophet Yūnus ﷺ.

This is also yet another *ḥadīth* which is much clearer where the Noble Prophet of Islām ﷺ has been quoted as saying:

لَيْسَ مِنْ قَوْمٍ تَنَازَعُوا (تقارعوا) ثُمَّ فَوَّضُوا أَمْرَهُمْ إِلَى اللهِ إِلَّا خَرَجَ سَهْمُ الْمُحِقِّ

> Not a single community has employed the act of drawing lots [when they are in a dead-end situation], by [first off] placing all their reliance upon Allah except that the drawing of lots of lands on what is the truth and manifests the reality [for them].[116]

Further details regarding this issue [of drawing lots] has been mentioned in the book, *Al-Qawāʿid al-Fiqhiyyah.*

[115] *Tafsīr al-Burhān*, vol. 4, pg. 37, trad. 6.

[116] *Wasāʾil al-Shīʿa*, Book on Passing Judgement, vol. 18, Section on the ruling on casting lots in determining a difficult affair, part 13, trad. 5.

Appendix II

Imam al-Sajjād ☻, Yazīd ibn Muʿāwiyah and Ṣalāt al-Ghufaylah

Did Imām al-Sajjād ☻ teach Yazīd ibn Muʿāwiyah the 'Secret' for the Latter to be Forgiven?[117 and 118]

There is a popular saying which states that: "History is written by the victors" and this holds true for Islamic history as well. In this regard, the following discussion seeks to clarify a misconception which is prevalent in the Muslim community about the spiritual power contained within Ṣalāt al-Ghufaylah.

As we have seen, there is no doubt that short of moving mountains, this prayer can completely transform an individual and move one from a life of sin to the path of righteousness. However, one needs to ensure that one does not get carried away in extolling the benefits of this or any other act of worship by misquoting narrations which have no historical or religious basis to them.

In regards to Ṣalāt al-Ghufaylah, some have mentioned that the fourth Imām, ʿAlī ibn al-Ḥusayn "Zayn al-ʿĀbidīn" ☻ also known

---

[117] Researched by **www.IslamQuest.net**, the original question and answer can be found at:
www. islamquest.net/fa/archive/question/fa14099.
We have translated it into English for the purpose of this book. (Tr.)

[118] Sayyid Muhammad Rizvi of the Jaffari Community Centre (**www.jaffari.org**) spoke about this alleged incident in detail on January 29, 2014. This lecture can be found at:
www.youtube.com/watch?v=8GfEmY0Deo4
from the 19:47 to 24:10 mark of the lecture. We have also included the excerpt of his talk in our video on Ṣalāt al-Ghufaylah found on our YouTube channel which can be found at:
www.youtu.be/tQZjlWk1ywI

as Imām al-Sajjād ﵇ taught the method of forgiveness to Yazīd ibn Muʿāwiyah after his heinous and atrocious crimes in Kerbalāʾ through this *ṣalāt*.

To clarify if this transpired or not, let us reflect on this supposed event and the response given by the scholars of Islām.

Question: In regards to the spiritual power and worth of *Ṣalāt al-Ghufaylah*, we have heard something to the effect that apparently Yazīd ibn Muʿāwiyah said to Imām ʿAlī ibn al-Ḥusayn al-Sajjād ﵇: "I have killed the son of the Messenger of Allah ... is it possible for me to still attain salvation?!" To this, Imām al-Sajjād ﵇ has been reported to have replied: "Yes, if you perform *Ṣalāt al-Ghufaylah*, then you will be redeemed." After this conversation transpired, Sayyida Zaynab binte ʿAlī said to her nephew, Imām al-Sajjād ﵇: "You are showing the means of salvation to the person who was directly responsible in the killing of your father!?" To this question from his aunt, the Imām replied: "All I have taught him is *Ṣalāt al-Ghufaylah*, however [I know that] Yazīd [due to him being hard-hearted] will never have the Divine succor *(tawfīq)* to perform this prayer."

Is this historical event true and if so, where is this event narrated (in which book)?[119]

---

[119] This event, as you will see, is a fabricated narration. The ʿArabic text of this can be found on numerous websites and has been recorded as below:

وكان مما روي في فضلها: أن يزيد بن معاوية لعنة الله عليه، سأل الإمام زين العابدين سلام الله عليه، هل لي من توبة وقد قتلت أباك أبا عبد الله (عليه السلام)؟ فقال له الإمام السجاد عليه السلام: نعم لك من توبة؛ وهي أن تصلي صلاة الغفيلة أربعين ليلة أو قال أربعين جمعة! فغضبت العقيلة زينب سلام الله عليها، وعاتبت الإمام السجاد سلام الله عليه؛ كيف يدلّ الطريد بن الطريد على طريق التوبة! فقال لها سلام الله عليه: لا عليك يا عمة، إنه لا يوفق لها.

Regarding the worth of it [*Ṣalāt al-Ghufaylah*], it has been narrated that Yazīd ibn Muʿāwiyah, may Allāh remove His mercy from him,

Answer: In researching those things which are frequently related and believed (to be true) by the masses, sometimes we come across issues which have been erroneously attributed to the infallible Imāms and are not found within their traditions and sayings.

Undoubtedly, *Ṣalāt al-Ghufaylah* is one of the highly recommended prayers for which there are numerous traditions[120] from the Imāms of the Ahlul Bayt, and it is based on such reports that all the jurists *(marājiʿ taqlīd)* have offered their verdicts *(fatāwā)* that this is a prayer which should be performed.[121]

However, regarding what has been mentioned in the above question regarding the level of merit which is contained in the performance of this prayer is not correct, and it must be noted that the details which formed the question do not appear in any of the reliable books of traditions, and there is nothing even remotely close to this contained in any of our books!

---

asked Imām Zayn al-ʿĀbidīn: "Is there any room for repentance *(tawbah)* for me, given that I killed your father, Abā ʿAbdillāh?" Imām al-Sajjād replied: "Yes, there is a way for you to make repentance and it is to perform *Ṣalāt al-Ghufaylah* for forty nights [and in some traditions, it is stated that the Imām said forty Fridays]!" [Upon finding out about what her nephew, Imām al-Sajjād had said], al-ʿAqīlah Zaynab [binte ʿAlī] became upset [at Imām Zayn al-ʿĀbidīn] and rebuked Imām al-Sajjād by saying]: "How can you possibly guide this fugitive and the son of a fugitive [Yazīd, the son of Muʿāwiyah] towards the course of repentance?" To this, he [Imām al-Sajjād] replied: "Do not worry my dear aunt! He will not have the [Divine] assistance needed to perform this [act of worship]."

120 The late Sayyid ibn Ṭāwūs, in his book, *Falāḥ al-Sāʾil* has mentioned numerous traditions regarding this recommended prayer. Please refer to page 244 of his monumental work.

121 Lankarānī, Muḥammad Fādhil, *Book of Ṣalāt*, pg. 54.

At this point, regardless of whether the details which are mentioned in the question are present or not in the books of traditions, if we were to merely study the contents of the question posed, we will see that from many points of view, it contradicts with the realities of the religion for the following reasons:

1. There is an inconsistency between the crime and the process of asking for forgiveness for it: One of the things which is agreed upon amongst the learned of the faith of Islām and is also an acknowledged fact among the principles of religion is that there must be a relationship between the crime and its punishment, or in this case, between the offense and the method of penitence. For example, if a person steals some money from someone, then as the religion of Islām has legislated within its teachings, the way that a thief will seek forgiveness is that one must return the wealth (or whatever was taken) back to its owner. If this is not possible, then some other way must be agreed upon which will satisfy the one who had his goods misappropriated. If a person had engaged in backbiting, then the method of seeking forgiveness entails one to either directly inform the person whom one spoke ill about and ask to be forgiven for the ill words spoken; but if this is not possible, then the person who engaged in the backbiting would have to pray to Allah ﷻ to forgive that person's bad deeds and to grant that person His goodness. Finally, if someone's reputation was ruined in the society, then the form of asking forgiveness for this major sin is that one must seek to reinstate the individual's position among those people. These are just some of the ways in which sins needs to be compensated for, however obviously there is much more which could be said in these regards [but we will not cover other instances here].

Of course, in many occurrences, Allah, the Grand, forgives the major sins through the performance of even minor acts of goodness, however regarding the issue at hand as was posed in the question, we see a huge lack of congruency between the crime and the way of making amends for it, and thus there is no way that we can bring forth a logical justification [for this event ever transpiring].

How is it possible that a person goes forth and sullies his hands in killing the Imām of the Muslims and that too the (grand) son of the Messenger of Allah ﷺ and is then told that the way for his sin to be removed is merely to perform *Ṣalāt al-Ghufaylah* and that his asking of forgiveness (in this method) will be accepted!?

How is it conceivable that a person like Yazīd ibn Muʿāwiyah who ordered the destruction of the City of the Prophet (Medina), and allowed his soldiers to attack and rape the women of that city or that such a person could make his way to Mecca and destroy the House of Allah ﷻ and then turn around and perform the *ṣalāt al-ghufaylah* and have all of his sins washed away!?

2. There are some people who claim that traditions exist which state that on numerous occasions in his life, Yazīd ibn Muʿāwiyah intended to perform *Ṣalāt al-Ghufaylah* as a means of asking for forgiveness from his despicable crimes, however because he had intense stomach pains, he was never actually able to perform this prayer.

We know that there is a credible and accepted tradition in which it is stated that the intention of an individual who simply intends to perform a good deed is even better than the good action intended.[122] This shows us that even if a person does not have the ability to perform a good deed, however if one had the intention to perform that action, then such an intention will actually be even greater and spiritually admirable than the performance of that good deed! Therefore, based on this tradition, if a person has the intention of repenting for one's sins, however does not get the opportunity to perform that specific act of asking for forgiveness

---

[122] Prophet Muḥammad ﷺ is reported to have said:

نِيَّةُ الْمُؤْمِنِ خَيْرٌ مِنْ عَمَلِه

The intention of a believer is even better than his action.

See al-Kulaynī, Muḥammad ibn Yaʿqūb, *Al-Kāfī*, vol. 2, pg. 84.

(in this case *Ṣalāt al-Ghufaylah*), then does this mean that his inner intention will not be accepted and that he will not be granted salvation from the acts of transgression which one had performed? Of course not! It is highly possible that there are some sins which a person performs by which one falls into the pit of spiritual darkness and through this, one loses the ability to even try and repent for one's sins.

In various traditions - which if we were to go into their details would require an entirely separate discussion - some specific sins have been mentioned which we are told that the performance of those evil deeds will prevent an individual from ever having the ability to ask for forgiveness. Some of these sins include the performance of actions which are considered as innovations *(bidʿah)* in the religion[123] - innovations which are not only performed by an individual, but even ones which many people may perform after which multitudes end up being deflected from the path of truth - throwing them into the valley of spiritual darkness and religious obscurity.

At this juncture, another question can also be posed: Principally, is it correct to say that such an individual (Yazīd ibn Muʿāwiyah and those like him) who suffered such an illness (that apparently he could not perform *Ṣalāt al-Ghufaylah* due to intense stomach pains) should be reprimanded due to his sickness? How is it possible that for other jurisprudential rulings such as fasting, pilgrimage to Mecca and other such acts which a person needs to have the physical means to perform for it to be considered an obligation, however if one is sick and is not able to, for example, carry out the fast because it is dangerous to one's health, then not only is it not obligatory to fast, but rather it will actually be considered forbidden for one to fast; however in regards to performing this recommended act (*Ṣalāt al-Ghufaylah*), if a person is not well and has a pain in a specific place in one's body (and this

---

[123] *Biḥār al-Anwār*, vol. 69, pg. 216.

is something which is out of one's control), that one should be blamed and not be forgiven (for one's past transgressions) due to something one does not have the ability to perform?

3. In this discussion, a statement has been attributed to Lady Zaynab binte ʿAlī which does not befit her status. In the "narration," we are told that after Imām ʿAlī ibn al-Ḥusayn al-Sajjād encouraged Yazīd ibn Muʿāwiyah to perform *Ṣalāt al-Ghufaylah* "so that his repentance for the killing of Imām al-Ḥusayn will be accepted," Lady Zaynab apparently objected to Imām al-Sajjād for giving this advice and said to him: "What, do you really intend to forgive the killer of your father!?"

How is it possible for one to conceive that Lady Zaynab, whose spiritual roots are planted in the family of revelation and is a woman who clearly knows and respects the station of Divinely-appointed Leadership *(Imāmah)*, would raise such an objection to her Imām - something which we may not even expect from a common person to do - let alone a woman of her status?

Yes, indeed it is possible that sometimes an infallible Imām or one of the saints of Allah may perform an act which may, at face value, look like they are going against the religious code *(sharīʿah)*, and if this was to occur then not only is it not a problem for a person to question or object to what they are doing and the reality of their actions, rather this is something which is acknowledged as being something which should be done. This has been seen in the event of the objections raised by Prophet Mūsā to al-Khiḍr in the story in which Prophet Mūsā accompanied al-Khiḍr in his journey.

In his travels, a point came when al-Khiḍr killed a young boy to which Prophet Mūsā protested that he had no right to kill an innocent child [and he was justified in raising this objection].

However, regarding the opposition which we are told Lady Zaynab levied against the Imām of her time, she is shown to have protested one of the actions of Imām al-Sajjād which is not appropriate on many fronts. First off, it was an action which was not expected from her as she believed that an infallible Imām would never show the worst human being the ways to felicity and the means to having his forgiveness accepted; secondly that Imām al-Sajjād ☀, who in his position as the Imām and then one who is the defender of the blood of Imām al-Ḥusayn ☀, has the right to forgive his murderer.

4. Another dilemma which this question poses is the reply which we are told was given by Imām al-Sajjād ☀ to his aunt, Lady Zaynab ☀, in which we are told that he said: "I said that Yazīd could be granted salvation through *Ṣalāt al-Ghufaylah*, however do not worry as he will never have the Divinely-granted ability to perform this prayer!"

In reality this is a form of enticement which the Imām used as he had been requested to show an act through which an individual may be forgiven for his sins, and the infallible Imām, despite knowing that Yazīd will not have the ability to perform it, still went ahead and encouraged him to perform this specific religious act of worship. In reality, it is entirely possible that if Yazīd actually felt true remorse for his actions, then Imām al-Sajjād ☀ would have guided him to perform some religious actions which he actually had the ability to perform so that he would have been absolved of his sins.

In addition to all of this, we know that throughout the life of Yazīd [after the events of Kerbalā'], he never once lamented for his actions in killing Imām al-Ḥusayn ☀ and his noble family and friends. Rather, his atrocities continued in the years after the tragic events of Kerbalā' in the disastrous event of *Ḥarrah*,[124] and

---

[124] One of the acts of sheer barbarity and inhumanity Yazīd brought down on the Muslims was the event of *Ḥarrah*. This incident resulted in the brutal killing of thousands of Muslims of Medina and was a massacre for which the order was issued by Yazīd ibn Muʿāwiyah himself. The deplorable atrocity of *Ḥarrah*, which blackened the pages of history, took place in the 63rd year of the

Islamic calendar during the reign of Yazīd ibn Muʿāwiyah between the powerful armies of the Levant (Shām) and the people of Medina. Yazīd gave the following order to Muslim ibn ʿAqabah, "Invite the people of Medina to pay allegiance to me - and do this three times. If they respond positively and pay allegiance, then let them go free. However, if they do not respond positively and refuse to pay allegiance, then fight them. If you triumph over them, then continue the massacre for three days. Anything that belongs to the city will be permissible for your army to loot. Do not stop the Levant army from doing whatever it wishes with its enemy. After three days, stop the killing and pillaging. Then again ask for allegiance from the people. They should promise to be Yazīd's slaves and servants. When you leave Medina, move towards Mecca for another attack and confrontation."

Ibn Qutaybah recounts that: "'The Shām army entered Medina on the twenty-seventh day of Dhū'l Ḥijjah in the year 63 AH. For three days Medina was plundered by the Levant army up to the appearance of the new moon of the month of *Muḥarram.*"

Following Yazīd ibn Muʿāwiya's orders, and after the seizure of Medina, Muslim ibn ʿAqabah told his soldiers: "Your hands are open and you are free to do whatever you want. You must plunder and loot Medina for three days." Thus, the city of Medina was subjected to wholesale murder and plundered by the Shām army. Everything was permissible for the Shām soldiers and no person remained safe from their harm. The civilians of Medina were killed and their property was looted. In this invasion of the Prophet's city, thousands of women were raped from which, thousands of children were born whose fathers were not known and these children later became known as 'the Children of *Ḥarrah* [*Awlād al-Ḥarrah*].'The streets of Medina were filled with dead bodies; blood flowed on the ground up to the Prophet's masjid; children were mercilessly killed in their mothers' arms; and elderly companions of the Prophet were exposed to torture and dishonour. The scale of therefore there is no proof that Imām al-Sajjād 🕮 ever showed such an individual, whose crimes continued to persist even after the tragic event of Kerbalā' the ways to seek forgiveness, or at least to a partial extent, exonerate him in the public sphere.

༄

This brings an end to the discussion on whether Imām 'Alī ibn al-Ḥusayn al-Sajjād 🕮 taught Yazīd ibn Mu'āwiyah how to perform *Ṣalāt al-Ghufaylah* or not - such that his repentance for the killing of Imām Ḥusayn ibn 'Alī 🕮 would be accepted.

From this we conclude that even though *Ṣalāt al-Ghufaylah* is as powerful as it is, and the fact that it holds such a prominent place in the teachings of Islām, this historical event has absolutely no basis to it and must be categorically rejected.

The readers are highly encouraged to follow the video link provided to gleam further knowledge on this important issue.

---

the killings was so great that because of his extravagance in killing the people, Muslim ibn 'Aqabah was from then onwards nicknamed *"Musrif"* ibn 'Aqabah, which in the Arabic language means 'the one who is extravagant.' After this horrendous event, the people of Madina wore black mourning clothes and the sounds of their weeping could be heard from their homes for up to one year.

Ibn Qutaybah narrates: "On the day of *Ḥarrah*, eighty companions of the Prophet were killed and after that day there was no *Badrī* (person that took part in the Battle of Badr) left. Seven hundred members of the *Quraysh* and *Anṣār* [the early Muslims who were local inhabitants in the city of Medina where Prophet Muḥammad and his family and companions migrated to] were put to death and ten thousand innocent people of the community were killed from among the Arabs, the *tābi'īn* (the generation of people who came after the companions of Prophet Muḥammad), and other virtuous people of Medina."

Appendix III

The Story of Prophet Yūnus (Jonah) in the Bible

Jonah Flees from the Lord

1 1 The word of the LORD came to Jonah son of Amittai: 2 “Go to the
great city of Nineveh and preach against it, because its wickedness
has come up before me.”

3 But Jonah ran away from the LORD and headed for Tarshish. He went down to Joppa, where he found a ship bound for that port. After paying the fare, he went aboard and sailed for Tarshish to flee from the LORD.

4 Then the LORD sent a great wind on the sea, and such a violent storm arose that the ship threatened to break up.

5 All the sailors were afraid, and each cried out to his own god. And they threw the cargo into the sea to lighten the ship. But Jonah had gone below deck, where he lay down and fell into a deep sleep.

6 The captain went to him and said, “How can you sleep? Get up and call on your god! Maybe he will take notice of us so that we will not perish.”

7 Then the sailors said to each other, “Come, let us cast lots to find out who is responsible for this calamity.” They cast lots and the lot fell on Jonah.

8 So they asked him, “Tell us, who is responsible for making all this trouble for us? What kind of work do you do? Where do you come from? What is your country? From what people are you?”

9 He answered, “I am a Hebrew and I worship the LORD, the God of heaven, who made the sea and the dry land.”

10 This terrified them, and they asked, "What have you done?" (They knew he was running away from the LORD, because he had already told them so.)

11 The sea was getting rougher and rougher. So, they asked him, "What should we do to you to make the sea calm down for us?"

12 "Pick me up and throw me into the sea," he replied, "and it will become calm. I know that it is my fault that this great storm has come upon you."

13 Instead, the men did their best to row back to land. But they could not, for the sea grew even wilder than before.

14 Then they cried out to the LORD, "Please, LORD, do not let us die for taking this man's life. Do not hold us accountable for killing an innocent man, for you, LORD, have done as you pleased."

15 Then they took Jonah and threw him overboard, and the raging sea grew calm.

16 At this the men greatly feared the LORD, and they offered a sacrifice to the LORD and made vows to him.

Jonah's Prayer

17 Now the LORD provided a huge fish to swallow Jonah, and Jonah was in the belly of the fish three days and three nights.

Jonah 2

2 1 From inside the fish Jonah prayed to the LORD his God. 2 He said:

> "In my distress I called to the LORD,
> and he answered me.
> From deep in the realm of the dead I called for help,
> and you listened to my cry.
> 3 You hurled me into the depths,
> into the very heart of the seas,
> and the currents swirled about me;

all your waves and breakers
swept over me.
4 I said, 'I have been banished
from your sight;
yet I will look again
toward your holy temple.'
5 The engulfing waters threatened me,
the deep surrounded me;
seaweed was wrapped around my head.
6 To the roots of the mountains I sank down;
the earth beneath barred me in forever.
But you, LORD my God,
brought my life up from the pit.
7 "When my life was ebbing away,
I remembered you, LORD,
and my prayer rose to you,
to your holy temple.
8 "Those who cling to worthless idols
turn away from God's love for them.
9 But I, with shouts of grateful praise,
will sacrifice to you.
What I have vowed I will make good.
I will say, 'Salvation comes from the LORD.'"

10 And the LORD commanded the fish, and it vomited Jonah onto dry land.

Jonah Goes to Nineveh

3 1 Then the word of the LORD came to Jonah a second time:

> 2 "Go to the great city of Nineveh and proclaim to it the message I give you."

3 Jonah obeyed the word of the LORD and went to Nineveh. Now Nineveh was an exceptionally large city; it took three days to go through it.

4 Jonah began by going a day's journey into the city, proclaiming, "Forty more days and Nineveh will be overthrown."

5 The Ninevites believed God. A fast was proclaimed, and all of them, from the greatest to the least, put on sackcloth.

6 When Jonah's warning reached the king of Nineveh, he rose from his throne, took off his royal robes, covered himself with sackcloth and sat down in the dust.

7 This is the proclamation he issued in Nineveh:

> "By the decree of the king and his nobles:
>
> > Do not let people or animals, herds or flocks, taste anything; do not let them eat or drink.
> >
> > 8 But let people and animals be covered with sackcloth. Let everyone call urgently on God. Let them give up their evil ways and their violence.
> >
> > 9 Who knows? God may yet relent and with compassion turn from his fierce anger so that we will not perish."

10 When God saw what they did and how they turned from their evil ways, he relented and did not bring on them the destruction he had threatened.

Jonah's Anger at the Lord's Compassion

4 1 But to Jonah this seemed very wrong, and he became angry.

2 He prayed to the LORD, "Isn't this what I said, LORD, when I was still at home? That is what I tried to forestall by fleeing to Tarshish. I knew that you are a gracious and compassionate God, slow to

anger and abounding in love, a God who relents from sending calamity.

3 Now, LORD, take away my life, for it is better for me to die than to live."

4 But the LORD replied, "Is it right for you to be angry?"

5 Jonah had gone out and sat down at a place east of the city. There he made himself a shelter, sat in its shade and waited to see what would happen to the city.

6 Then the LORD God provided a leafy plant and made it grow up over Jonah to give shade for his head to ease his discomfort, and Jonah was very happy about the plant.

7 But at dawn the next day God provided a worm, which chewed the plant so that it withered.

8 When the sun rose, God provided a scorching east wind, and the sun blazed on Jonah's head so that he grew faint. He wanted to die, and said, "It would be better for me to die than to live."

9 But God said to Jonah "Is it right for you to be angry about the plant?"

"It is," he said. "And I'm so angry I wish I were dead."

10 But the LORD said, "You have been concerned about this plant, though you did not tend it or make it grow. It sprang up overnight and died overnight.

11 And should I not have concern for the great city of Nineveh, in which there are more than a hundred and twenty thousand people who cannot tell their right hand from their left - and many animals?"

Glossary of Prophets and Saints

Throughout the book, to maintain continuity, we have employed the ʿArabic names of the Prophets and saints of Allah - just as they have been used in the Qurān and *aḥādīth.* We mention their English equivalents here:

ʿArabic Name	English Equivalent
Ādam	Adam
Ayyūb	Job
Dāwūd	David
Hārūn	Aaron
Ibrāhīm	Abraham
Ilyās	Elias or Elijah
ʿIsā	Jesus
Isḥāq	Isaac
Ismāʿīl	Ishmael
Khiḍr	There is no equivalent in English for this saintly individual
Lūṭ	Lot
Muḥammad	Muḥammad
Mūsā	Moses
Nūḥ	Noah
Sulaymān	Solomon
Yaḥyā	John
Yaʿqūb	Jacob
Yasaʿa	Elisha

Yūnus	Jonah
Yūsuf	Joseph
Zakariyyā	Zechariah

Index

Image Credits

1. **Front cover image:**

shiaarts.ir/sa/download/DBF16C720F6AE1A9129A25F8AC94B9D3.jpg

2. **Back cover image:**

glenpoolchurchofchrist.com/sermon-archive/jonah-preaching-repenting/

3. **Arabic Calligraphy in introduction:**

2wf.org/there-is-no-deity-except-you-exalted-are-you-indeed-i-have-been-of-the-wrongdoers

4. Actions in the Prayers:

Illustrations designed by Sr. Jennah Heydari – jennah@revertmuslims.com

Other Publications Available

1. *A Land Most Goodly: The Story of Yemen in the Quran and in the Times of Prophet Muḥammad and Imam ʿAlī ibn Abī Ṭālib* by Shaykh Jaffer Ladak
2. *A Mother's Prayer* compiled and translated by Shaykh Saleem Bhimji and Arifa Hudda
3. *A Star Amongst the Stars: The life and times of the great companion: Jabir ibn Abdullah al-Ansari* by Shaykh Jaffer Ladak
4. *Alif, Baa, Taa of Kerbala* written by Shaykh Saleem Bhimji and Arifa Hudda
5. *Arbāʿīn of Imam Ḥusayn* compiled and translated by Shaykh Saleem Bhimji
6. *Contentious issues in Islamic History – ʿUmar ibn al-Khaṭṭāb* written by Saeed Dawari and translated by Shaykh Saleem Bhimji
7. *Deficient? A Review of Sermon 80 from Nahj al-Balāgha* by Ayatullah al-Uzma Shaykh Nasir Makarim Shirazi and translated by Shaykh Saleem Bhimji
8. *Exegesis of the 29th Juz of the Qurʾān – a Translation of Tafsīr-i Nemuneh* by Ayatullah al-Uzma Shaykh Nasir Makarim Shirazi and translated by Shaykh Saleem Bhimji
9. *Foundations of Islamic Unity* – an English translation of *Al-Fuṣūl Al-Muhimmah Fī Taʾlīf al-Ummah* written by

ʿAbd al-Ḥusayn Sharaf al-Dīn al-Mūsawī al-ʿĀmilī and translated by Batool Ispahany

10. *Fountain of Paradise – Fāṭima az-Zahrāʾ in the Noble Quran* written by Ayatullah al-Uzma Shaykh Nasir Makarim Shirazi and compiled and translated by Shaykh Saleem Bhimji
11. *God and god of science* by Syed Hasan Raza Jafri
12. *House of Sorrows* written by Shaykh ʿAbbas al-Qummi and translated by Aejaz ʿAlī Turab Ḥusayn Hussayni
13. *Inspirational Insights* by Mohammed Khaku
14. *Islam and Religious Pluralism* by Ayatullah Shaykh Murtadha Mutahhari and translated by Sayyid Sulayman ʿAlī Hasan
15. *Journey to Eternity – A Handbook of Supplications for the Soul* compiled and translated by Shaykh Saleem Bhimji and Arifa Hudda
16. *Knocking on Heaven's Door* compiled and translated by Shaykh Saleem Bhimji and others
17. *Love and Hate for Allah's Sake* by Mujtaba Saburi translated by Shaykh Saleem Bhimji
18. *Love for the Family* compiled and translated by Yasin T. Al-Jibouri, Shaykh Saleem Bhimji and others
19. *Moral Management* written by ʿAbbas Rahimi and translated by Shaykh Saleem Bhimji
20. *Morals of the Masumeen* written by Arifa Hudda
21. *Prayers of the Final Prophet – A collection of supplications of Prophet Muḥammad* written by ʿAllamah Sayyid Muḥammad Ḥusayn Tabaʾtabaʾi and translated by Tahir Ridha-Jaffer
22. *Ramaḍhān Reflections* compiled by A Group of Muslim Scholars and translated by Shaykh Saleem Bhimji
23. *Salat al-Ayat* written by Shaykh Saleem Bhimji

24. *Ṣalāt al-Ghufaylah: Salvation through Patience & Perseverance* written by Shaykh Saleem Bhimji
25. *Secrets of the Ḥajj* written by Ayatullah al-Uzma Shaykh Ḥusayn Mazaheri and translated by Shaykh Saleem Bhimji
26. *Sunan an-Nabī* written by ʿAllamah Sayyid Muḥammad Ḥusayn Taba'taba'i and translated by Tahir Ridha-Jaffer
27. *Tears from Heaven's Flowers: An Anthology of English Poetry about the Ahlulbayt* by Abrahim al-Zubeidi
28. *The Day the Germs Caused Fitnah* by Umm Maryam
29. *The Firmest Armament: Commentary on Āyatul Kursī (The Verse of the Throne)* written by Sayyid Nasrullah Burujerdi and translated by Shaykh Saleem Bhimji
30. *The Last Luminary and Ways to Delve into the Light* written by Sayyid Muḥammad Ridha Ḥusayni Mutlaq and translated by Shaykh Saleem Bhimji
31. *The Muslim Legal Will Booklet* by Shaykh Saleem Bhimji
32. *The Pure Life* written by Ayatullah al-Uzma as-Sayyid Muḥammad Taqi al-Modarresi and translated by Shaykh Jaffer Ladak with commentary by Dr. Zainali Panjwani and Shaykh Jaffer Ladak
33. *The Third Testimony: Imam Ali in the Adhan* compiled and translated by Shaykh Saleem Bhimji
34. *The Torch of Perpetual Guidance - A Commentary on Ziyārat al-ʿĀshūrā'* written by ʿAbbas Azizi and translated by Shaykh Saleem Bhimji
35. *Weapon of the Believer* written by ʿAllamah Muḥammad Baqir Majlisi and translated by Shaykh Saleem Bhimji

...And many more to come, God-Willing

www.ingramcontent.com/pod-product-compliance
Lightning Source LLC
LaVergne TN
LVHW041322080426
835513LV00008B/554